# A Basic G
# Building
# Cross-Country
# Fences

Philip Herbert

Drawings by Johnny Marsh

© Philip Herbert 2000

Edited and produced for The Pony Club by Barbara Cooper

Design: Alan Hamp
Photographs: Philip Herbert and Andrew Guinness
Drawing on p10 courtesy of HSE Books

Published by The Pony Club
NAC Stoneleigh Park
Kenilworth, Warwickshire
CV8 2RW

Printed in Great Britain by Westway Offset, Wembley

ISBN 0-9537167-2-4

# Contents

# Illustrations

*The author, on site, with personal Land Rover*

# Introduction

This book includes enough information to enable anyone with little or no experience of cross-country course construction to go out and start work on fences. Some basic advice on course design is provided, but if you are contemplating building a course from scratch, I suggest that you seek expert advice.

I have been a full-time professional course builder for more than twenty years. During that time much has changed and much has stayed the same. The main difference now is that the size of materials used is far bigger, necessitating mechanical handling. Many construction techniques are the same as they always were, but some have been altered and refined, and I have endeavoured to include all the new methods.

Between the time of writing the manuscript of this book and its publication there have been dramatic happenings in the sport of Horse Trials world wide. In 1999 there were several fatal accidents to riders on cross-country courses. This brought the sport under very close scrutiny by the governing bodies. Although there was no consistent pattern in the fatalities it was decided that all aspects of cross-country course design and construction should be reviewed. A working party chaired by Lord Hartington, a distinguished horseman, and including experts from within and outside the sport, was set up to report on what could be done to improve safety. This book is the first to be published since the report was made public.

The committee interviewed individuals concerned with all the different aspects of cross country courses, including representatives of the Pony Club. They recommended that:

- Statistics of all falls should be recorded.
- Rider training and qualifications should be closely looked at.
- Officials should be appointed at events to prevent competitors from riding recklessly.
- The highest level of medical cover should be available at competitions.
- Helmets and body protectors should be of approved specification.
- The intensity of efforts incorporated into a course should be fore most in the minds of course designers and inspectors so as not to ask an undue question of the horse.
- The state of the ground should be given careful consideration before a competition.

Among other considerations was the viability of deformable fences.

Course builders should at all times have the safety of the horse and rider at the forefront of their minds. Try not to think in the old fashioned way, 'We need a fence to sort them out'. The course has to be balanced to give a challenging ride to the best competitors without overfacing the less experienced ones.

There are bound to be more recommendations and changes to the rules of the sport in the near future, and further editions of this book will be updated accordingly. Meanwhile I hope that it will encourage and help you to go out and build safe and inviting obstacles that will prove to be of benefit to riders, horses and the sport in general.

Philip Herbert
*Glapthorn, 2000*

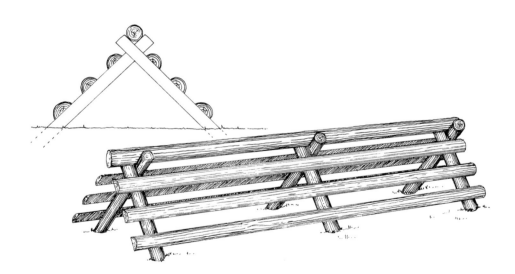

# 1 Equipment

## 1 Basic Tools

There are many different aspects to course-building, ranging from simple flagging of fences and stringing off the course, to complicated ground and water works. A wide variety of tools, machinery and equipment will be required to carry out the full range of tasks.

The average garden shed or garage should contain enough kit for you to help with just basic setting-up tasks. At the very least you will need a claw hammer, spade, sledge hammer and a pair of pliers. If you are going to get involved with actually building fences, a few more tools will be needed. These should include (as well as the above) chainsaw, crow bar, jemmy, shovel, fencing pliers, twisting bar, Surform, and measuring sticks.

## 2 Clothing

You cannot work efficiently if you are cold, wet or uncomfortable. Take sensible clothing with you. Wellingtons are not safe to work in; they offer no protection to your toes or instep, and if you are sawing they fill up with sawdust. Sturdy boots with steel toe caps and open tread soles are best.

If you are going to be using a chainsaw you must have special chainsaw boots, which protect your feet from the saw chain, as well as protective chainsaw trousers, gloves and helmet with visor and ear defenders.

Other items needed are waterproof trousers and coat and a stout pair of gloves. Do not wear loose items, such as scarves, which can get caught in machinery or materials. When wearing a tie, tuck the loose end safely inside your shirt.

In the summer it is advisable to use sun block, particularly if you are not accustomed to being out of doors; it is surprising how quickly newly exposed skin becomes burnt.

If you are painting – particularly creosoting – wear a boiler-suit-type of overall and rubber gauntlets to cover all your clothes and bare skin; creosote burns your skin and the effect is magnified by the sun. Wear a hat without a peak, as wide-brimmed hats stop the vapours from rising and can cause face irritation.

You will probably be out in the open for a whole day at a time with your vehicle as your only shelter. Take a Thermos flask containing a hot drink; sandwiches; and high-energy snacks such as chocolate. In the summer take plenty of water to drink, also in a Thermos flask, as it is much more pleasant if kept cool. You should also have a good first aid

*1. The recommended protective clothing for those using chain saws*

*SAFETY HELMET*
*Conforming to BS5240 (replace in accordance with manufacturer's instructions – normally every 2-3 years).*

*HEARING PROTECTION*

*EYE PROTECTION*

*CLOTHING*
*To be close fitting (protection incorporating loosely woven long nylon fibres or similar protective material is recommended for the shoulders, neck, arms and upper chest area).*

*GLOVES*
*With protective pad on the back of the left hand.*

*LEG PROTECTION*
*Incorporating loosely woven long nylon fibres or similar protective material (all round protection is recommended for tree surgeons and occasional users).*

kit and a mobile phone to summon help in the event of an accident and to ring for advice if you have a problem.

Course-building can be great fun and brings twofold job satisfaction – firstly from making a tidy job of whatever you are working on, and secondly if the fences jump well.

# 3 Vehicles

If you are thinking of course-building on a professional basis, you will need a much more comprehensive set of equipment, starting with a vehicle. This should preferably have four-wheel drive as you are bound to find ground conditions that are too difficult for ordinary cars, and trying to get about with spinning wheels will damage the ground and make an unsightly mess. The wider the tyres, the more lightly the vehicle will tread, causing the least compaction to the ground and helping to preserve the going in the best state for the horses at all times: a vitally important factor.

An open-backed vehicle, such as a pick-up, is most convenient and safe. If you carry tools, materials, and dangerous liquids such as petrol, creosote and weed-killer, in the back of a van or estate car, and have an accident, you are likely to find yourself upside down with all your

*CHAINSAW BOOTS*
*Incorporating protection for the toes, top of foot and front of lower leg (alternatively protective gaiters worn in combination with steel toe capped safety boots are*
*acceptable for occasional users working on even ground where there is little risk of tripping or snagging on undergrowth or brush).*

equipment on top of you and petrol soaking into your trousers. With a pick-up you are safely separated by the cab from anything you are carrying and from the smell of petrol or creosote, but you can easily reach over the side to get at anything you need. It may be necessary to devise some storage boxes to keep things dry and for security purposes –

particularly as most course builders stay away from home quite often and have to park in public places.

A trailer will also be more or less essential for transporting materials and large machinery or equipment. A low-load type, with the wheels underneath and drop sides, is the most useful as it can easily

*2. Course builder's vehicle and trailer*

be loaded by a forklift, and small tractors can be driven on to it. If long poles are to be carried, the trailer must be long enough so that they do not overhang the back more than the legal limit for your local roads. However, trailers which are too long will continually dig their back ends into the turf when driving over undulating ground.

It is extremely dangerous for the trailer to be loaded so that the back is heavier than the front, as this tends to lift the back of the towing vehicle, making it unstable and liable to jack-knife.

# 4 Chainsaws

The next most important requirement is a suitable chainsaw. One with an engine size from 40cc to 60cc and with a bar length from 12" (30cm) to 20" (60cm) is about right. If the saw is too small it will struggle to do the work; if too large, you will struggle to work it.

Always choose a well-known make so that spare parts are easy to get hold of wherever in the world you may be working, as breakdowns are common. If you cannot afford a new saw, buy from a dealer who can offer a warranty – not from an auction. Chainsaws are extremely dangerous and should be treated with great respect. In the UK it is compulsory by law to wear a full set of safety clothing when using one. This includes boots, trousers, gloves and helmet with visor and ear defenders. If you have never used a saw before, go on a training course run by an Agricultural College or Agricultural Training Group.

You will also need a full kit of files and tools for sharpening and maintenance.

# 5 Small Hand Tools

**Pen-knife.** Strong and sharp for cutting rope and string. Should be carried at all times in your pocket, especially during competitions when it may be needed in a hurry to extricate a cast horse.

**Claw hammer.** The heavier the better, and preferably with a steel shaft. The claw should only be used to pull out the smallest of nails.

**Fencing pliers.** A multi-purpose tool for cutting, twisting and holding wire or rope; also used for extracting staples.

**Twisting bar.** A length of 1/2" (12mm) steel rod, about 12" (30cm) long, for twisting wire tight.

**Surform or rasp.** For removing sharp edges of timber and whiskers left by the saw.

**Pocket tape measure.** At least 10' (3m) long.

**Long tape measure.** 15m-50m (16yds"– 55yds).

**Bolt cutters.** Large enough to cut nails.

**Large adjustable spanner.**

**Stillsons.** To hold seized bolts.

**Timber tongs.** For picking up heavy timber that you cannot get your fingers underneath.

**Small flat jemmy bar.** For levering off light rails and removing small tacks.

**Hacksaw.** For cutting bolts.

**Screwdrivers, spanners and socket set.** For carrying out running repairs.

*3. Small hand tools.*
*Top row: timber tongs, adjustable*
*spanner, stillsons, hacksaw, rasp.*
*Bottom row: wire cutters, fencing*
*pliers, twisting bar, claw hammer,*
*small jemmy, short and long*
*tapes.*

# 6 Large Hand Tools.

**Fibreglass or tubular shafts** are very expensive but are best on long-handled tools, as they are almost unbreakable. A broken shaft in the middle of a busy day can be a real source of hold-up, losing both time and money.

**Spade.** A stainless steel one is best if you can afford it, as soil does not stick to it as firmly as to ordinary steel.

**Shovel.** The long handled, pointed-end type lends itself very well to course-building.

**Crow bar.** About 5' (150cm) long, with a chisel on one end and a point at the other for making pilot holes for stakes and general levering jobs.

**Ground rammer.** For compacting loose soil and hard-core.

**Turning lever.** For rotating heavy, round timber and for straightening twisted posts.

**Long jemmy bar.** For removing large nails and levering timber apart.

**Fencing mall.** With its flat head for knocking in stakes, this is better than a sledge hammer, as the head does not damage the stakes so badly. If its head is made of cast iron it should not be used for hitting anything other than wood, as it might shatter. Malls with aluminium and rubber heads are rather bulky to carry around.

**Light sledge hammer.** For general hitting duties such as knocking in very small stakes, and for fence dismantling.

**Long-handled pruners.** For removing low branches and cutting birch and fence dressing materials.

**Stout garden shears.** For trimming brush fences and apron dressings.

**A 9' (3m) tow chain.** With a hook on one end and a ring on the other, for dragging materials and pulling out posts.

**One or two 'D' shackles.** For attaching the chain to tractors, etc.

**High-lift jack.** This is an extremely useful tool (and also an extremely dangerous one.) There are various makes, of which the best is probably the Canadian 'Jackall', available from firms who specialise in off-road vehicles. It can be used for raising a top rail to height and holding it there for fixing; pulling out a post; compressing birch; or even winching out or jacking up a bogged-down vehicle. **Warning.** This machine is very unstable when raised high, and may fall over sideways. When you are operating the lever which switches the mechanism from up to down, or vice-versa, make sure that the main lifting handle is up: if not it may fly upwards violently and catch the operator under the chin.

A pair of these jacks can make very light work of what is the heaviest job when building a fence.

**Measuring sticks.** Essential for everything except the most basic schooling fences. The rules of all competitions state that obstacles must be measured from the point where a horse takes off, not vertically. Therefore you will need a long, straight edge with a spirit level attached, to reach from the take-off point, at least 4' (1.2m) away from the fence, and up to 10' (3m) away if the fence has a large spread or a ditch in front of it.

There is no purpose-built instrument available in the UK at present, so it is necessary to make your own. Alloy tube is the best material, as it does not warp like wood and is lighter to carry around than steel. As it is very difficult to find tubes which will fit inside each other, you should make your own portable telescopic instrument. You will also need a measuring stick graduated in inches or centimetres, to read off the height, which can be bought from a tool shop. The single-fold type lasts longer than the multi-fold, which seems to get broken very easily. An alternative is to pin the metal inner tape of a pocket tape-measure

4. Large hand tools.
Top row: sledge hammer, mall, crow-bar, post hole tamper, Shuv-holer, shovel, spade, jack.
Bottom row: rake, pruners, small turning lever, large turning lever, mattock, axe, long jemmy.

to a suitable piece of wood; it needs to be long enough to measure the maximum drop of the biggest fence that you are likely to build.

UK Jockey Club Course Inspectors use an optical device for measuring fences, but it is awkward to handle, particularly with small fences, and is very expensive.

# 7 Power Tools

The most common power tools are powered by electricity. It is illegal in the UK, as well as dangerous, to use 240-volt equipment out of doors; you will often find yourself working in or over water, or in the rain, and 240-volt electricity and water do not mix! Power tools for hire will be 110-volt. Though larger and heavier, they comply with the law and are safer.

The most useful tool is a large cordless drill, which can drill holes up to 1" (25mm) in wood and ½" (12mm) in steel. It can also be used as a screwdriver; screws are very useful: especially for obstacles which have to be dismantled soon after they have been built. It is much easier to remove a screw with a mechanical screwdriver than to pull out a nail. The battery should last for most of a day's work, but it is a good idea to carry a spare.

The next best option for drilling holes is a chainsaw engine with a drill attachment. This is very powerful and will drill holes of any size. As it takes a few minutes to fix, it is easier to have it on a separate engine from the one which you use for sawing. An old saw engine without modern safety features is fine for this. Purpose-built petrol-engined drills are now available; one with a reverse gear is best.

A heavy duty petrol hedge-cutter is useful for birch and other brush fences. It must be of the most robust design available, as birch is very hard to cut. If you will not be using it all that often, you can easily hire one.

If a tractor is not available and if the ground you are working on is straightforward, a petrol-powered post hole borer is an option. These machines can make holes up to 8" (20cm) in diameter, but for large holes they may need two people to operate them. In hard or stony ground either they will not go in or they become stuck in the hole and can be very difficult to extract.

*5. Power tools. Top: petrol engine drill. Centre: petrol chainsaw, battery drill. Bottom: hedge cutter. Right: petrol engine post hole borer.*

# 8 Heavy Machinery

Course-building involves moving and working with heavy and awkward materials, but various machines are available which make many of the hard grafting and lifting jobs much easier and which also save a lot of time.

## Tractors

Many modern tractors are huge, as they are designed for rapid cultivation work. They are not very suitable for course-building, because they are cumbersome to manoeuvre and the cabs are inconveniently high off the ground. They are also very heavy, and cause a lot of compaction to the ground.

**Compact and garden tractors** are generally too small to be practical. They can be unstable when lifting loads on steeply sloping ground, and they are not able to tow a large enough trailer. Something from 25 to 70 hp is best and may be light enough to carry around on a trailer behind a four-wheel drive vehicle. Older tractors are often preferable as they tend to be easier to use and to repair. They also either have no cabs or basic ones which offer better visibility. As you will not be in the cab for long periods of time, weather protection matters little. Also, you will be doing a lot of manoeuvring about where there are other people standing around and working, and it is essential for you to be able to see, and also to hear directions from assistants. The modern closed-in cabs make it very difficult to hear what is going on outside. If you consider buying an older tractor, choose a well-known make: it

will be easier to obtain spares for it. Make sure that it comes with all its ancillary equipment: drawbar, top link, stabilisers to stop the link arms swinging from side to side, and a safety roll bar if there is no cab.

**Four-wheel drive** is a useful feature, especially if you have a front-end loader, though these tractors are less manoeuvrable than ones with only two-wheel drive, and they can cut the ground up more readily. The wider the tyres on a tractor the better, as they are kinder to the ground, especially when front-end loaders are fitted.

The two other essential items of machinery are (a) one for lifting and (b) one for helping to put posts in the ground.

(a) A **front-end loader**, with a bucket to handle earth and stone, is a great asset; it can pick up a heavy timber load and position it. On smaller tractors it is advisable to have some ballast – e.g. an implement or a concrete block – fitted to the back to counterbalance the weight. A two-wheel drive tractor under 35hp with a loader fitted will struggle to lift very heavy loads, will have little traction when it does, and may be unstable.

(b) Implements for putting posts in the ground come in two forms: **borers** and **drivers**.

**Post-hole borer.** This is a large auger driven by the tractor's power-take-off. It will drill a post-hole up to 4' (1.2m) deep, and will work well in soft clay or loam-type soils. On very hard or stony ground it may have difficulty biting in, and may leave a residue of spoil in the hole which will need to be cleared out by hand afterwards.

When a post-hole has been bored and the post has been put in the

hole, the soil has to be manually shovelled back and compacted very firmly – quite a time-consuming task. Note Be very careful to stand clear of the rotating auger, and keep all loose clothing well away.

**Post-driver.** This is generally considered to be better than a borer. It is basically a giant hammer which hits the post into the ground, and all the operator has to do is stand and watch it. Posts thus fixed are always firmer than those in dug or bored holes.

Post-drivers need to be treated with the greatest respect, as serious injury can be inflicted by them. For example, whatever you are doing, get into the habit of never putting your hand on top of a post; you are then less likely to put it there without thinking, and ending up with it crushed.

Be particularly careful when driving small stakes into hard ground with a heavy post driver. The stake may snap in half and fly towards you.

It is essential to use a machine that has an efficient mechanism for gripping the post. Several different makes are available, and the best are probably those of Antipodean origin, as they have the heaviest weights and will drive really large, blunt posts, into hard ground while holding them safely. Also, they are operated from the ground alongside the machine – rather than from the tractor seat, which can lead to accidents because of communication problems between the driver and the helper on the ground.

A **tipping trailer** is useful for moving earth and hard-core and can also be use for transporting timber and brush.

6. *Tractor and post driver.*

7. *Tractor and post hole borer.*

For keeping the ground in good condition a **mower** may be needed. An **aerator** which has spikes for making holes in the ground to relieve compaction and encourage good turf growth is also a great asset.

For earthworks and water obstacles, some form of **digger** will be required. These are easy to hire, complete with driver. To get the best value for money (by keeping the hired machine working all the time) you have to be well organised.

The most common type of digger, usually referred to as a 'JCB', (although this is only the name of one particular make), has front-loader arms with a bucket and a back-hoe digger on the back. JCBs are heavy machines with large stabiliser legs, and if the ground is anything but rock hard the legs sink down as far as 1' (30cm) – which is most undesirable right in front of a fence.

Used by an unskilled operator a JCB can do a lot of damage and make a lot of mess in a short space of time. A **tracked mini-digger** is probably better, as long as you do not turn it too sharply. It is much kinder to the ground and is more versatile, as the boom can swing round through 360 degrees, which is particularly useful when building water obstacles. The disadvantage of mini-diggers however, is that they are very slow when travelling over long distances. They also have incredibly expensive transmission systems which on older machines are prone to giving problems.

It is also possible to obtain **agricultural back-hoe diggers** for fitting onto conventional tractors. If you need to carry other implements on the tractor they take a long time to mount and de-mount, but they can be a good option as they are less expensive when not in use. In course-building you will need the digger for a while, then you will need to do some timber work, and then you will need the digger again. With a suitable bucket fitted, a back-hoe digger can be used for sinking post-holes, though holes that it makes tend to be much bigger than those made with an auger and they require a lot of filling in and firming up.

Popular on farms these days are **purpose-designed rough terrain forklifts**: very handy machines which can lift up to 2.5 tons (2500kg), and are useful for moving tree trunks and portable fences. They can scoop up 2 tons (2000kgs) of sand or stone, carry it to where it is needed, then tip and spread it (as long as the ground is dry). They are very heavy, and if not driven with care can damage the ground. They nearly always have four-wheel drive; those with four-wheel or articulated steering are less likely to do damage than those with rear-wheel steering only. The telescopic versions can be very unstable and should only be driven by an operator who is old enough and who has passed an appropriate test under UK laws.

A **self-propelled dumper** is better for moving earth and hard-core than a tractor and trailer, as it is very manoeuvrable, and can get into awkward places, leaving the tractor free for loading it. These vehicles are highly recommended for water obstacles, and are readily available for hire.

# 2 Basic Design

## Layout of Track

In order to build a cross-country course for Pony Club hunter trials or one-day events, a site of not much less than 75 acres (30 hectares) will be required, to allow room for the course and for parking, tents, dressage and show jumping. With luck the site will include some interesting features, and will be all grassland and well drained. Features to look out for are hedges, ditches, slopes, banks, clumps of trees and some natural water. Possibly the most important requirement is a co-operative and helpful landowner or tenant farmer. Whoever is farming or grazing the land will be considerably inconvenienced when the course is in use, and will have to move livestock to other fields.

Try to obtain a large-scale map of the site. Use this to plan the basic layout of parking and other activities, then to see what land is left for the course. The distance must fit into the limits laid down in the rules for whatever competitions are to be run.

Calibrate a piece of string from the scale of the map to the mid-way length allowed, then fit this round the obvious features on the map – to get a preliminary idea of where to go.

Factors to consider at this stage are collecting ring, warm-up area, start and finish. The latter should leave the horses with at least 100 meters in a straight line to pull up safely. It is very bad for a horse's legs to pull up very quickly or to turn sharply after a long gallop.

In an ideal world, the first two fences should take the horse back towards the horseboxes, to encourage the more novice animals to get off to a good start.

A control point will be needed, from which the maximum number of fences can be seen. Any fence out of sight of the control point will need a radio link, to report on the horses' progress and to summon help in the event of an accident.

Every fence must be accessible to vehicles, not only for construction purposes but also so that emergency vehicles can reach it.

If you have not designed a course or fences before, consider calling in professional help. As fences are expensive to build, it is very important to get them right first time. A good course will be favourably received by competitors and they will come back to your event year after year. A bad course will put riders off and, even when it has been improved, it will take a long time to tempt them back.

At this stage it is time to walk round the course for the first time. Don't set out with a large committee, as the focus of attention will be bound to shift to other subjects.

Designing on one's own can be hard work; two or three people are necessary for ideas to be bounced back and forth.

Walk the whole course, to get the feel of it. Try to establish where most of the fences will go, and confirm the start and finish area. Check the distance with a measuring wheel.

Do not worry if the whole course is not designed after the first walk-round. Go away and sleep on it and come back a few days later for another look. You will then find that other ideas come easily to mind.

It does not matter if every fence is not designed by the time construction starts. The more time you spend on the site, the more familiar you will become with it, and the more and better ideas you will come up with.

Try to incorporate as many of the interesting natural features as possible: they are much cheaper to use than artificial ones. Make the course as varied as you can, to keep it interesting and to ask many different questions of horse and rider.

First and foremost the fences must be *safe,* with no traps or tricks built in to catch the competitors out, and with nothing that can hurt a horse unduly if he makes a mistake.

The fences must be solid and durable: the more solid a fence looks, the more a horse will respect it; the better it will jump; and the longer it will last. Flimsy fences built from light materials will not be respected, will jump badly, will probably get broken, and will not last very long.

The condition of the take-off and landing of each fence is very important. It should, as far as possible, be in the same condition for the last horse in the class as for the first. Under certain conditions the ground may have to be made up.

Try to incorporate questions into the course to test the rider and the team trainer as much as, if not more than, the horse or pony. For the Pony Club, 'L' fences must be provided near to the more difficult main obstacles, to allow the less experienced competitors to complete the course without being eliminated.

## Siting of Obstacles

More bad fences are created by being poorly sited than by poor construction. The same fence design in more than one different situation can create a completely different test. Think long and hard before deciding on the final site for an obstacle. Walk the line from the previous fence to the next one, and make sure that it flows and does not have any uncomfortable sharp turns for the horse.

Avoid steep slopes in any direction. Horses find it easiest to jump with a slight uphill approach. The trouble with these fences is that the way in which the rules require them to be measured tends always to make them look small.

Upright fences can be jumped going uphill and on the flat, but never with a downhill approach.

Fences with a downhill approach can be designed to *look* very high but should hardly ever be the maximum allowed. They should always slope well away from the horse as it jumps. Steeply-sided slopes can cause horses to slip, particularly in wet ground conditions. Gently sided slopes are acceptable but not for complicated or combination fences.

Do not build fences near to gateways, water troughs or farm tracks, where the ground may look fine when it is very dry, but after heavy rain and farm vehicle or animal activity can be badly poached.

Look out for stumps and roots which may be hidden by vegetation and

23

8(a). *Measuring sticks. A long, straight edge with spirit-level attached, and an upright stick graduated metrically or in inches*

which only become apparent when the undergrowth has been cleared for the course to be jumped.

Be wary of the bright green marsh grass that grows in wet areas. Wherever it is found the ground is liable to be very soft. Although this may not be apparent when you are walking on it, the weight of a horse may soon go through a crust of dry material into bog underneath.

If there are a number of natural hedges on the site, try to use them, as they make very inviting obstacles. Most hedges will be too big to jump in their natural state. Simply cutting them down to size will not work, as you will be left with a row of large stumps as big as a man's arm and totally unsuitable. They will have to be correctly cut and laid, which is a specialist and expensive operation, so make sure that this is allowed for at the initial planning stage.

## Measuring Heights and Distances

This is an important aspect of all courses, particularly nowadays, when many accidents are investigated and there may be a resulting insurance claim. If an obstacle is found not to comply with the rules for the competition because it is either too high or too wide, or the drop is too great, there could be very embarrassing questions to be answered in a court of law.

The height of a fence must be measured from a point where the average horse would normally be expected to take off. Make sure that you have a good levelling stick which is both long enough and straight enough, and an upright measure that is accurate.

Horses always take off farther away from a fence than most people think. They can take off closer to a fence that slopes away from them than they can to an upright. They tend to get nearer to fences approached uphill than down. They can take off right up to the edge of an open ditch.

Go and look at the hoof-marks on a course after a competition. Study all the different types of fences and from them learn how far away from a fence to measure.

Check that the fence measures throughout its width span, not only in the middle. The spread must be measured from the outside edges of the top rails, not from the tops. The drop should be measured to where a horse will land, which could be a considerable distance away; again, only experience will tell you where.

There is nothing to be gained by the course builder trying to pull the wool over the eyes of the course inspector.

## Roping

This is one of the most fundamental and important operations in fence building. As well as being essential from the safety angle, correct neat roping can enhance not just individual fences but also the overall appearance of the course.

The most practical type of rope is polypropelene, ¾" in circumference or 6mm in diameter. Tools you will need are a pair of fencing pliers and a sharp pocket knife.

*(Step-by-step illustrations are on the next two pages.)*

25

8b-1

8b-2

8b-3

8b-4

8b-5

8b-6

8b-7

8b-8

8b-9

8b-10

8b-11

8b-12

# 3 Materials

The thickness of the top rail of a fence is what a horse first looks at when he approaches. The deeper this is and the less daylight showing underneath it, the better the horse can see it. As a general rule, if you can pick up the top rails comfortably by hand they are not big enough! When ordering top rails, specify 7" to 8" (175mm-200mm) top diameter: i.e. at the small end. It cannot be stressed enough how important it is to build fences from substantial timber, which determines how the fences look and jump, and how well they stand up to hard use.

## Timber

### Size
It is preferable to have the timber delivered in 24' (8m) lengths and to cut it yourself into the various sizes. The largest and straightest can be kept for top rails, and the others – which may not be so straight or may have been damaged in handling – can be cut up for posts and dummy posts. There is no such thing as a completely straight tree! It is up to the skill of the course-builder to make the timber look as good as possible.

### Choice of timber
Some types of tree last better than others. European Larch is the best, followed by Red Cedar. Norway Spruce, Corsican Pine and Scots Pine have the shortest life span. Norway Spruce grows the straightest but tends to taper a lot, which is a disadvantage if very long poles are required. Scots Pine has rather unattractive bark and lumpy knots and does not grow very straight. Corsican Pine looks almost exactly the same as Larch. Be careful that an unscrupulous dealer does not try to sell you this by claiming that it is the more valuable timber.

### Pressure treatment
This is a process in which the timber is peeled, dried and placed in a tank. The tank is then sealed and a chemical preservative is pumped in under high pressure which forces it into the wood. When this has been efficiently carried out, and the poles have been cut, it should be possible to see how far the preservative has penetrated. Some types of tree accept the chemical better than others: the most important factor being that the timber should be really dry before treatment. Simply dipping it in or painting it with preservative has very little effect compared to the correct process: which will ensure that the timber lasts at least 15 years. It may be possible to obtain a certificate guaranteeing this.

**Round poles** are the timbers most used for cross-country fences – for rails, posts and dummy posts. They can be found in different forms: rustic, as felled, with the bark still on; or peeled, with the bark removed; or peeled and pressure-treated with preservative to prevent rotting; or re-cycled (such as telegraph poles, which are treated with creosote.)

**Rustic poles** are the most plentiful and probably the cheapest to buy. Their availability depends on where you live. The first places to try are large estates or sawmills. If they cannot help you they may be able to put you in touch with a contractor working in the woods, who is the most likely person to have this type of timber for sale. Start looking for it well before you need it, and never buy it without inspecting it first: your idea of what constitutes a top rail may differ from that of a woodsman's. Most people think that the only fences horses jump are showjumps and you therefore want that type of pole!

The price will probably be quoted in cubic feet or even tons. Try to get this converted into a per-pole price, and remember that delivery and VAT will probably not have been added.

Ask the haulier to be as careful as possible with the timber-loading grab, so as not to damage the bark too much.

Rustic poles look very good when newly cut, but after a year or two the bark starts to fall off and they begin to look untidy. Small knots that were covered by the bark will now need to be removed. At this stage they can be peeled and creosoted or stained to smarten them up. Any rustic timber which comes into contact with the ground will start to rot after 3 to 5 years. Timber which is off the ground will last 7 to 10 years.

**Re-cycled timber** such as telegraph poles and railway sleepers/railroad ties are pressure-treated with creosote to a very high standard. They can last for decades and can be used over and over again for a variety of fences. If you can find them at the right price they are invaluable.

In some areas, telegraph poles can be bought at the roadside, direct from the gangs who take them down, by doing a deal with the foreman. In other areas all the poles are taken to the central depot or to a dealer and are harder to come by as well as expensive. Note that the poles may have an assortment of ironwork, nails and wires on them, which are time-consuming to remove.

If you are using expensive telegraph poles, you may find that it is cheaper to buy off-the-shelf round, treated fencing strainers for posts than to cut up the valuable long poles which cannot be obtained so readily.

Railway sleepers/railroad ties can sometimes be seen at farm sales or other auctions. They are usually in stacks of about nine. Move all the sleepers and have a good look at the bottom ones. You can be sure that the best will be on the top, hiding the bad ones. Otherwise you can buy them from dealers, but they are so expensive these days that for most of the relevant work it is probably better to spend your money on new timber.

Re-cycled creosoted sleepers often have nails, screws and grit embedded in them, which can do a lot of damage to your saw. Also, the sawdust is impregnated with creosote, which can be unpleasant – particularly in hot weather, or if you get some in your eye.

**Half-round agricultural fencing rails**, which are almost always pressure treated are very useful for cladding and revetting. There are two types: natural finish, which are simply split poles ,tapered and not necessarily straight. More user-friendly are the machined ones which are turned and smoothed into an even shape with no bends or taper; they fit tidily side by side with no gaps. These can be purchased from most agricultural or fencing merchants as can other standard fencing materials which may well be needed, such as half round stakes and sawn fencing rails. Heavier sawn timber can be bought from sawmills and builders' merchants. Remember that it will probably not be pressure-treated and should therefore not be used below ground.

## Slab Wood

This is a by-product available at sawmills. It is the first slice which comes off the log when it goes into the mill and is flat on one side and slightly curved (usually with its bark on) on the other. It is often quite cheap and is useful for cladding palisades, etc. Nowadays local sawmills are usually so efficient that the slabs may be very thin and flimsy and not really strong enough for course-building purposes. However, they vary from mill to mill, so some good slab wood may still be found.

## Brush

This is important for dressing and for making steeplechase-type fences and artificial hedges. The most common brush comes from the twigs of the silver birch tree, grown from stumps which have been coppiced or cut off at ground level. Silver birch grows only in sandy soils, so the brush is not found everywhere. As it is used for racing fences, your local racecourse or point to point clerk of the course should be able to tell you where to find it. It comes tied in easy-to-handle bundles about 6' (2m) long, but when handling it do not wear a woollen sweater as the twigs will snag and ruin it. The bundles can vary considerably in size, so be sure to find out the sizes before comparing prices.

Before being transported, the brush must be roped or strapped down very tightly. It is so springy that strappings soon come loose; so stop and check it after the first few miles. The bundles on top of the load must have their butt ends towards the front – otherwise the wind will lift the twiggy ends up and fold them back. Birch will last up to three years in the open; much longer if kept dry. Always store it under-cover and consider protecting birch fences with a strong tarpaulin or tin sheets.

The main other type of brush consists of branches of fir trees left on the ground to rot after the trees have been felled. These can usually be obtained for nothing from foresters – but when collecting it be sure not to interfere with their work. In the cool months it will stay green for several weeks, but in hot weather it will wither in a matter of days.

## Stone

This is needed in ground work for infilling. If it will be coming into contact with the horses' feet it should be no larger than 3/4" (20mm) and mixed with a small proportion of dust. The type of stone depends on the geology of the particular area. One of the best materials available in Britain is the soft yellow stone found on the Limestone Belt (Northamptonshire, Lincolnshire, Cotswolds, etc.) This can be crushed under the heel of your boot, so is least likely to hurt a horse. Pinky-grey limestone and granite are much harder, and it may be necessary to blind over them with dust or sand to protect the horses.

# Fixing materials

These consist of a range of nails from 4" (100mm) to 8" (200mm). Nails up to 6" (150mm) can be easily obtained. The 8" (200mm) ones are not so easy to find. They are very useful to a course-builder as they will go through a sleeper or a large half-round rail. In the UK they are made in small batches, and tracking them down may involve a few calls to the larger fencing and fixing suppliers. For staples 1½" (40mm) is the only size needed.

Wire for revetting should be No 8 gauge (4mm) and soft; it is impossible to bend or twist high-tensile wire, which is more commonly used for fencing. Smaller gauge wire can be used for fixing dummy posts but when twisted it is more likely to break than the heavy duty version.

For tying rails onto posts, use ¾" circumference or 6mm diameter polypropylene rope. White looks the smartest, but be careful, as some white rope is not resistant to ultra-violet light and quickly breaks down. It is on sale at rope and twine suppliers.

Instead of using wire to fix dummy posts it is customary nowadays to have 'pins' made. These are 12" (30cm) long by ½" (12mm) round steel rods with a washer welded on to one end, in effect giant nails. They are knocked into a hole which is drilled slightly shorter than their length so that they grip tight. They have other uses as well as for fixing dummy posts, and any engineering firm or blacksmith should be able to make them for you.

For more complex fixings, use studding or threaded rods in ½" (12mm) diameter x 1m lengths. With these you can make your own bolts by putting a nut on either end.

For temporary fixings and fence numbers use cross-head screws with a battery screwdriver; they are much easier to remove than nails.

In the UK, creosote is the most practical product for smartening up fences and comes in light and dark shades. Be particularly careful when using it, especially in hot weather. Always wear overalls, gloves and goggles, and do not carry it in a car or van, only in an open-back vehicle or trailer. Also available now are various wood stains in many different shades, but note that some water-based products will not work on rustic timber.

# 4 Fences

## 1 Post and Rail Variants

Professional cross-country course-builders always refer to the results of their labours as 'fences' or 'obstacles'– never 'jumps' which they consider to be gaily-painted objects that fall down when hit by a horse.

An island fence, that is to say one that is in the middle of a field rather than in a fence line, should be at least 18' (5.5m) wide, and even then should probably have wings. A fence in a fence-line, unless specifically designed to be narrow like a stile, should be at least 15' (4.5m) wide. The wider the fence the more inviting it will be to a horse, and if the going is wet the width will provide more ground for the damage to be spread over, making it fairer for the horses competing later in the day.

The most common ingredient of all cross-country courses is the plain post and rail fence. It is the one single type of construction that you will find yourself building more than anything else. It can be a straightforward fence on its own, and should only be used at the beginning of the course; it can be augmented to make several other fences; or it can make up the elements of a combination fence.

To build the most basic fence you will need:

1 top rail
1 lower rail
3 posts
3 top rail dummy posts
3 lower rail dummy posts
rope
wire or pins

Lay the top rail on the ground exactly below its prescribed position so that the siting can be checked. Go back to the previous fence and walk the line from this to the fence that you are about to build, over the rail, then on to the next fence. See if the route flows well without too many changes of direction. If it doesn't, consider moving the rail to a better site. Make sure that the take-off and landing are reasonably level, with no holes or sharp bumps or any other feature that might cause an extra problem for the horse. On side slopes, the fence will look best if the bigger end of the rail is pointing downhill. Time spent checking at this stage is never wasted.

When you are satisfied that all is well, it is time to put in the two outside posts. If you are using a post-driver, back your tractor up to the rail and knock in the posts about 8" (20cm) from the end of the rail. When digging or boring holes, dig out a turf where the posts are to go and then roll the rail out of the way. By doing this you can ensure that the posts will never be too far apart for the length of the rail. Drive the posts

*9. Post and rail stages: (a). Top rail laid on ground exactly below eventual height, with outside posts in place.*

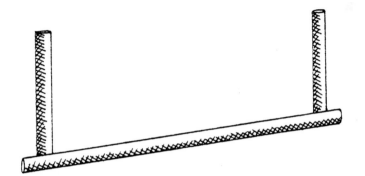

removed, bring it in from the landing side, so that you can look at the fence and measure it easily. The tractor will affect your view of the fence, as it will obscure the landing, and if it is left standing for a long time with a heavy weight on the front wheels, they may sink down and leave a rut.

Measure the height and check that it complies with the rules for the class in question. Even when it does, the fence may still be too high. You must stand back, look at it intently, and ask the opinion of any one helping you to make sure when it is right – raising or lowering the rail accordingly. If you are using a rustic rail it will almost certainly not be straight, but you can twist it round to make it look better; if you do this be extremely careful. Only rotate the bottom of it towards the post –

to the required depth or, having dug or bored the holes deep enough, put only about 6" (15cm) of spoil back into the hole and ram it firm with a rammer or the end of a stake. Repeat this until the hole is full, then shape the turf that you first dug around the base of the post.

Getting rustic posts upright is best done by eye rather than with a spirit level; there is not usually a straight edge on which to put the level. Look at the first post from different angles, then line the second one up with it. When they are both firmly fixed, the rail can be raised. If you are digging or boring, make the hole for the middle post at this stage, but do not fix it – and be careful not to fall in the hole!

If you have a tractor and loader, or a forklift, it is safest to use it to lift the rail up and then to put the rail on props or high-lift jacks. If no props or jacks are available, which means that the tractor cannot be

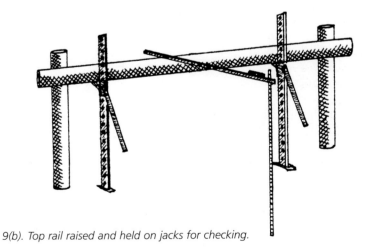

*9(b). Top rail raised and held on jacks for checking.*

otherwise it will fall straight off the props or jacks – and use a turning lever, so that you have enough leverage. The safest and most satisfactory method is to lower the rail to the ground, carefully rotate it until it looks right, then raise it again. As soon as the correct height has been reached, secure the rail with rope to at least one of the posts. A rail on props or jacks is extremely unstable. It could easily fall on its own or when nudged while fixing, and could hurt someone, damage tools, and cause a lot of extra work in repositioning it.

When you are happy that the rail is correctly positioned, it can be fixed firm. Dig out a turf about 10" (25cm) square and about 4" (10cm) deep in front of both posts. Measure from the bottom of this hole to the underside of the rail. Cut a length of timber at least half the diameter of the top rail to the length measured (dummy post) and

fit it in position. To do so it may be necessary to raise the rail slightly, which should be possible with a jack, without loosening the ropes, but take care. If you do raise the rail, make sure that it goes down to the same height again. If it doesn't, cut the dummy shorter or dig some more soil out of the hole. Then fix the dummy with wire or a pin.

The wire must be soft, not high-tensile, and should be at least 3mm in diameter. Measure round the post and dummy, which is easiest done with a piece of string. Double the string and cut the wire about 15" (40cm) longer than the length measured. Bend it in two and put it round the post and dummy about 8" (20cm) below the rail. Pass a short bar through the loop end and twist it round the two free ends until it is tight. Cut off the two spare ends, staple the loop down, and also put staples in either side of the post to tighten and tidy it further.

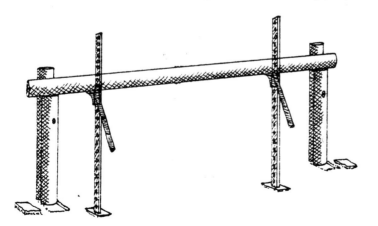

*9(c). Top rail dummy post installed.*

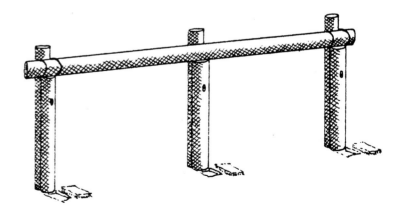

*9(d) Centre post with dummy installed.*

To fix with a pin use a 12" (30cm) x $\frac{1}{2}$" (12mm) pin and drill a hole $\frac{5}{8}$" (16mm) in diameter and 10" (25cm) deep through the dummy into the post, about 8" (20cm) below the rail. Put the pin into the hole and drive home the last 2" (5cm) with a sledge-hammer.

The advantages of pins over wire are that they are quicker to fit, as you do all the work from the front of the fence; they prevent the weight of the rail from pushing the dummy down into the soil; and when you have finished with the fence the pin can be recovered and used again.

When both dummy posts have been fitted, it is as well to rope the rails securely to the posts. Use $\frac{3}{4}$" circumference (6mm diameter) polypropeleyne rope which can be fed out from a coil or reel. (1) Splice a loop at the end by passing the rope four times through one lifted strand. (2) Stand behind the post. Pass the looped end of the rope over the top of the rail on the left of the post, under the rail and round the back of the post, under the rail on the right of the post and over the top of the rail back towards you. (3) Cut the rope off with about 3' (1m) spare. (4) Pass the cut end through the loop, pull it tight, and knot it with a half-hitch. Keep the knot to the right hand side of the post. (5) Pass the free end behind the bottom strand through the gap between post and dummy, and pull it across until it is below the knot. (6) Take the end and pass it over the top strand through the gap between post and dummy on the left of the post, and down behind the bottom strand. Pull it across until it is next to the knot. (7) With a pair of fencing pliers, pull the end sharply downwards. You will have created a mechanical advantage device like a pulley system which will draw the top and bottom strands together and tighten them. (8) When the two strands have met, continue to pass the free end of the rope over and behind the strands as before, pulling the end tight. This will lash the rope all the way across the back of the post. (9) Cut off the tails of the rope.

The middle post or posts can now be fitted. If you have a rail that is at all bent you will probably see that the middle post is quite out of line with the end ones, which is why you shouldn't put it in until the rail is positioned. Fix a dummy post and rope as described above.

A post and rail fence, no matter how small, is incomplete without a lower rail: which can be full-round or half-round. Round rails present a better, more ascending shape, which is the most inviting for a horse to jump, but they take slightly longer to fit. Half-rounds make the timber go further, as long as you have some efficient way of splitting them, but they do not make such an inviting fence.

If you are buying the timber from a sawmill it may be possible to

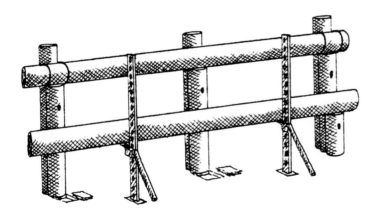

*9(e) Lower rail offered up on jacks.*

have some of the rails split into half-rounds on the band or circular saw, which can only cut down absolutely straight poles. This means that the best of your load will not end up as top rails. As all mills can't split up to 24' (7.5m) lengths, it is preferable to split the poles yourself with a chainsaw – which can follow any bends in the timber thus using the slightly flawed poles.

(1) Prop the chosen rail up on wooden blocks about 1' 6" to 2' (45cm to 60cm) off the ground and rotate it so that from the side view it is a straight as possible.

(2) Use wedges or cut 'Vs' in the blocks to stop the rail from rolling.

(3) Stand on the left hand side of the pole and with a very sharp chainsaw score a line down the centre of the pole from end to end – about 1" to 2" (25mm to 50mm) deep, keeping the bar as near to horizontal as possible. This will help you to keep an even line following the curves of the pole. (4)When you get to the end, turn the bar of the saw vertically and use the top to cut back down the line that you have made all the way through the pole. You will thus be able to see that the bar is following your pre-cut score mark.

This operation takes time, practice and patience. Once the pole is cut in half you will find that it can, if necessary, be bent to fit onto the fence.

Position the lower rail and hold it on jacks or props. It should sit at about half the height of the top rail; use your eye to gauge when it is correct rather than measuring it. If the fence is quite small, be careful that the gap between top and lower rails is not such that a horse's leg could go in easily but not come out easily. If it is, lower the rail, even if it is almost on the ground. It will look best slightly lower than half-height anyway. Remember: safety is the most important consideration.

A round lower rail can be fixed in exactly the same way as the top one,

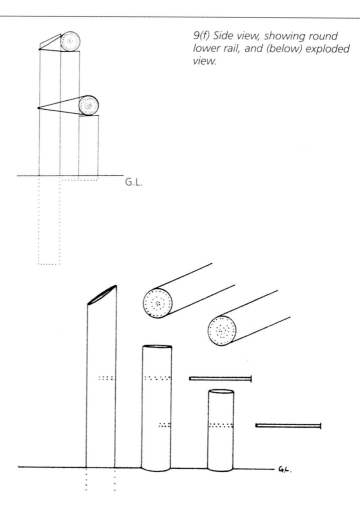

9(f) Side view, showing round lower rail, and (below) exploded view.

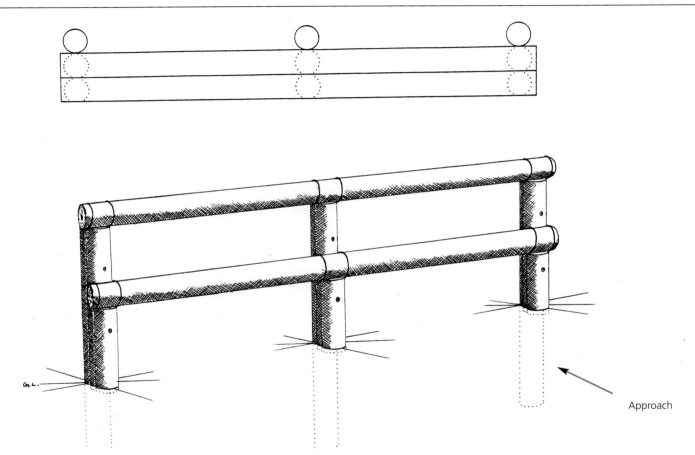

Approach

*9(g) Completed upright post and rail fence. (Top) Seen from above.*

10. *Splitting a rail.*

but if there is any danger of a horse getting trapped in the fence, rope the rail only at one end. A half-round can be nailed at one end and held with a chock at the other; an 8" (200mm) nail may be needed. The chock can be made out of an offcut of half-round rail cut to form a 'V' in which the rail will sit. Nail the chock to the dummy post, but be careful not to split it if it is quite short. Should you be in doubt, find a longer offcut that goes right down to the ground. If a horse's leg goes behind it, the rail will fly out of the chock and can easily be replaced by the fence judge.

Saw the tops of the posts off at an angle sloping down towards the landing side of the fence. At this stage be careful not to cut the ropes, as it is more difficult to tie them after the post tops have been cut off. The angled top will allow rain water to run off and will ensure that there is very little chance of the horse catching it.

Cut off the ends of the rails tidily, all the same length. It does not matter if the rails overhang the posts by quite a few inches, as long as both ends of each rail look the same. It is wasteful to cut a lot off the rails as they may be used again for another fence.

Rasp the cut ends with a Surform to make them less sharp, and remove the whiskers left by the saw. Stand back and check that all is neat and tidy and as safe as possible.

*The advantages of this method of construction are:*
• It is very strong, as the force of a horse hitting the fence will be taken directly onto the side of the posts.
• The fence has the inviting, ascending shape which is most comfortable for a horse to jump, because the lower rail is on the front of the dummies.
• If a horse becomes cast on the fence with its forelegs on one side and its hind legs on the other, anyone with a penknife can cut the ropes so that the rail can be rolled onto the ground to free the horse. All fence judges should have a knife!
• If very large and heavy timber is used, and as long as the cast horse is not in distress, it is better to wait until the course-builder arrives before attempting to dismantle the fence, as there is a risk of the horse or a human being hurt by the falling rails.
• If the fence is found to be too big it is easy to alter the height. A slice can be cut off the top of the dummy post and the rail will drop down without the need for re-tying the ropes. If a large adjustment is made it may be necessary to cut off the tops of the posts as well. The rail can even be raised, as long as the posts are high enough, by putting a block on top of the dummy: though this looks rather untidy. It is better to replace the dummy, or to jack it up and put a block under it.
• It is advisable to use pins, so that when the fence is dismantled no nails or staples will be left in the timber, making it difficult to use again.

*The disadvantage of this method* is that the fence can be jumped in only one direction.

The old fashioned way of building a rail fence was to cut a 'V' in the top of the post, sit the rail in it, then secure it by stapling wire over the top. With this method, wire cutters were needed to extricate a cast horse, and the weight of the horse could make it difficult to get the rail down. This type of fence is difficult to adjust and not very strong, as the back of the post can split away.

Plain rails can also be built from sawn timber. These fences tend to be very upright and uninviting to jump and should be sited where the horse can approach only at a steady speed: e.g. right at the beginning of the course or after a sharp turn. The top rails should be at least 5" (125mm) deep and preferably 6" (150mm). They are best made out of fencing posts with the 5" or 6" side facing frontwards.

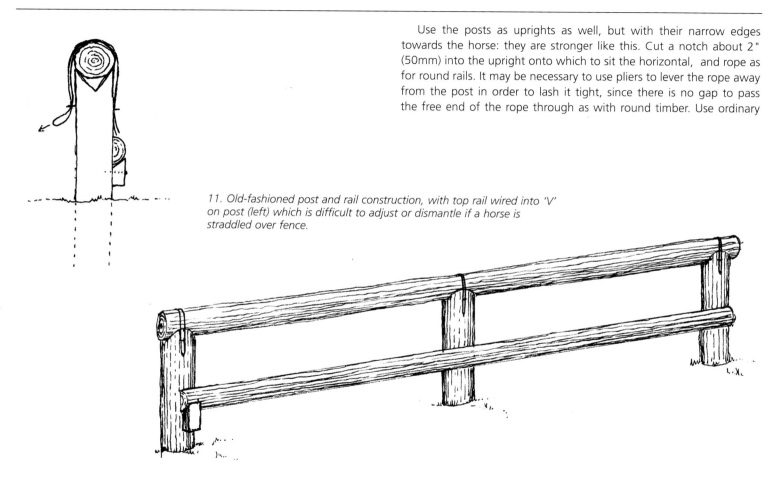

Use the posts as uprights as well, but with their narrow edges towards the horse: they are stronger like this. Cut a notch about 2" (50mm) into the upright onto which to sit the horizontal, and rope as for round rails. It may be necessary to use pliers to lever the rope away from the post in order to lash it tight, since there is no gap to pass the free end of the rope through as with round timber. Use ordinary

*11. Old-fashioned post and rail construction, with top rail wired into 'V' on post (left) which is difficult to adjust or dismantle if a horse is straddled over fence.*

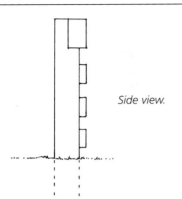

*Side view.*

$3\tfrac{1}{2}$" x $1\tfrac{1}{2}$" (90mm x 40mm) fencing rails underneath; depending on the height, you may need two or three. Nail them to the front of the uprights at regular intervals. Use only one 4" (100mm) nail through each rail into each post, so that if necessary it will be easier to dismantle the fence. If the gaps between the rails are such that a horse's leg will go into but not come out of them easily, use fewer rails.

*12. Sawn post and rails with top rails made from the same timbers as the posts, and with standard fencing rails beneath.*

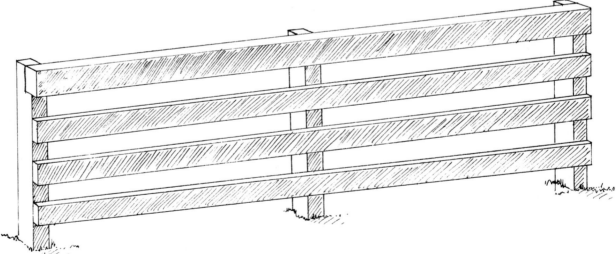

Now that you have mastered the basic construction technique, other more complex fences can be built using the same method.

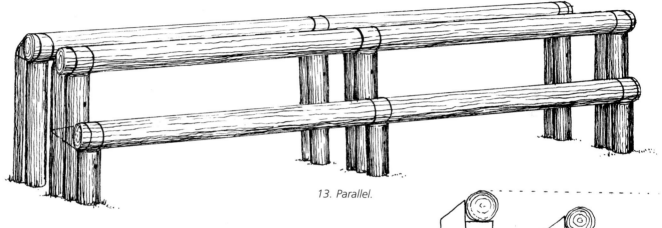

*13. Parallel.*

A **parallel** is simply two plain post and rails, one behind the other. The back rail should always be 1" to 2" (25mm-50mm) higher than the front rail so that it can be clearly seen by the horse on approach. There should never be a lower rail on the back section of a parallel.

This fence can be useful for a competition where two different classes have to use the same course. The back rail can have posts only at its ends and slightly wider apart than the front rail. For the smaller class only the front rail should be used. For the bigger class the back rail is lifted into position and quickly roped on to make a higher and wider fence.

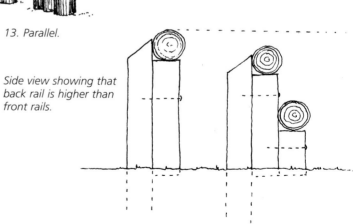

*Side view showing that back rail is higher than front rails.*

*14. Triple bar with 3 rows of posts.*

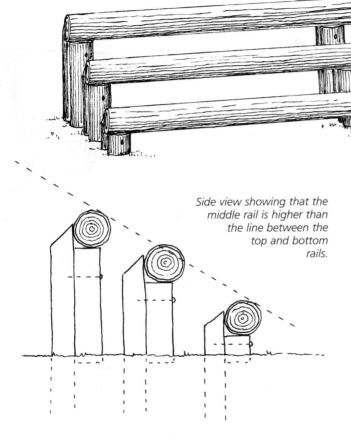

*Side view showing that the middle rail is higher than the line between the top and bottom rails.*

A **triple bar** is three post and rails set in ascending order. When building this type of fence do not be tempted to use the maximum base-spread allowed for the class. If the base-spread is too great it can encourage a horse to 'paddle' in the fence: that is to say to try and put his legs between the poles, which would result in a nasty fall. It is a fault that can occur with any fence with a large base-spread and no top-spread. The base must be kept in proportion to the height; only experience will teach you when this is right.

The top of the centre pole must be in line with, or higher than, a line between the top of the bottom pole and the top of the top pole. The lower or front pole must be either touching the ground or high enough so that a refusing horse's leg cannot slide underneath it and become trapped.

Another way to build a triple bar is to make a plain post and rail, and fit struts to the top of the dummy posts, going down to and dug

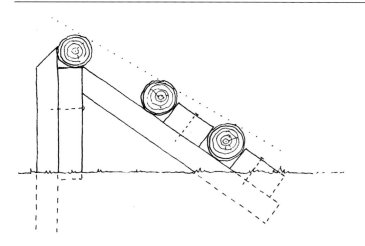

A **shark's teeth** is a post and rail fence with angled teeth fixed to the top rail – or, better still, to the top of the dummy posts going down to the ground at angles in front of the fence. If the posts are fixed to the top rail they must be far enough apart at the top for a horse's leg to slide through the gap and not be caught. They should be roped, but if you nail them use small nails so that if a horse is cast on the fence it can easily be dismantled. As with a triple bar, the base-spread should not be too great: no more than the height of the fence. If it is correctly built this is another easy and inviting fence to jump.

*15. Triple bar with struts, showing lower rails held in position by blocks.*

into the ground at an angle in front of the fence. The lower two rails then sit on the struts and are anchored by blocks nailed, bolted or wired to them. This method is not as flexible for adjusting the fence but is probably better for very small obstacles. The correctly built triple bar is a very inviting fence to jump and should cause very little trouble.

16. *Shark's teeth*

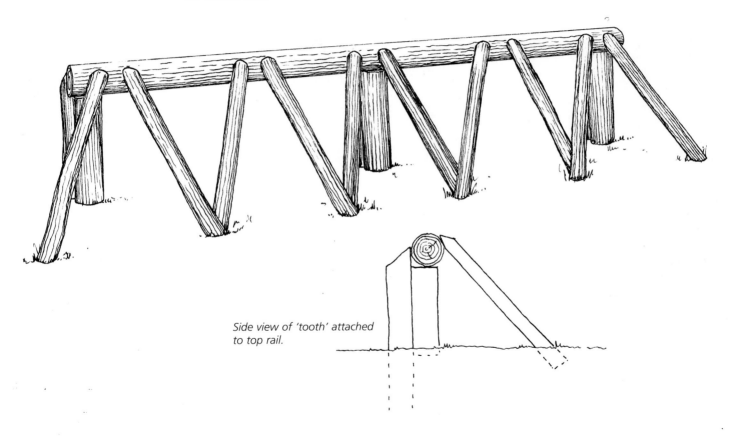

*Side view of 'tooth' attached to top rail.*

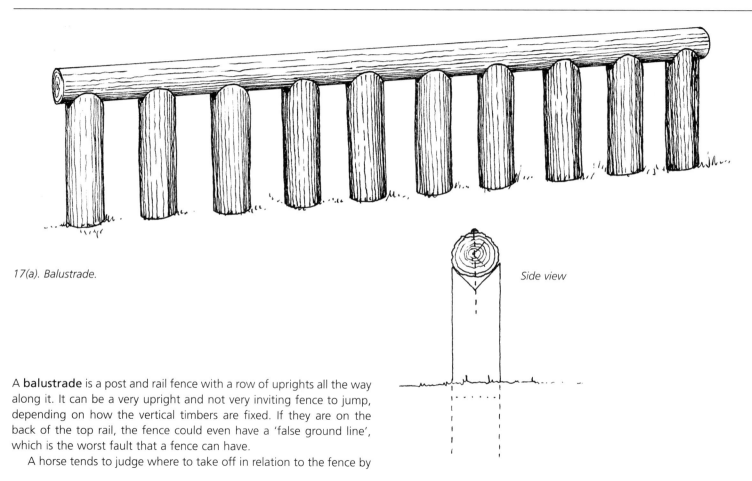

17(a). Balustrade.

*Side view*

A **balustrade** is a post and rail fence with a row of uprights all the way along it. It can be a very upright and not very inviting fence to jump, depending on how the vertical timbers are fixed. If they are on the back of the top rail, the fence could even have a 'false ground line', which is the worst fault that a fence can have.

A horse tends to judge where to take off in relation to the fence by

*17(b). Balustrade, showing false
ground line without lower rail.*

looking into the bottom of it. If the bottom of the fence is further away from the horse than the top, the horse will almost always hit the fence, which is extremely dangerous. A showjump built like this would be knocked down by every horse. It is important therefore to build fences with an ideal ascending shape, to make it easy for the horse to judge where to take off.

A **Helsinki steps** is a set of rails built in sections across a sloping piece of ground. On a shallow slope the downhill end of one rail may be set on top of the uphill end of the next. On steeper slopes a block may be needed to provide sufficient difference. Make sure that the measurements of as much as possible of each section are within the rules. Do not use a spirit level to set the rails. If you do they will give an illusion of being higher than horizontal at the downhill end, and will almost certainly be over height. Set them by eye.

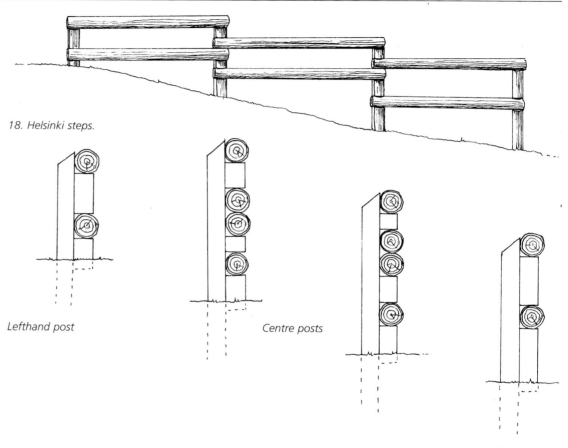

18. Helsinki steps.

*Lefthand post*

*Centre posts*

*Righthand post*

A **zig zag** can have varying numbers of sections but needs at least four to look the part. When designing one of these fences it is very important to lay the rails out on the ground before putting the posts in. Be careful not to make the angles too acute: they must be more than 90 degrees if the fence is to jump comfortably. At the back, the rails will be on the wrong side of the posts unless two posts are put in. With only one post the construction is not very strong, as the weight of a horse hitting the fence is taken by the rope. To overcome this, use the rope double, and replace it every year.

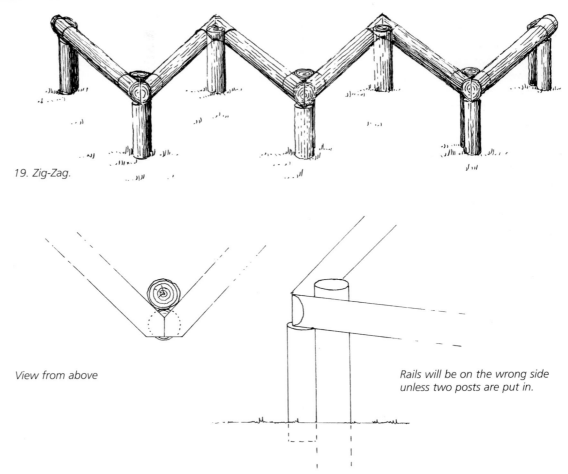

19. Zig-Zag.

*View from above*

*Rails will be on the wrong side unless two posts are put in.*

A **palisade** is a post and rail which has been completely clad in underneath with vertical boards or half-rounds. First build a plain rail with no lower rail. As it will not be possible to dismantle this fence there is no advantage in roping the top rail on; it can be bolted, wired, or a stout half-round can be used and nailed on. Dig a trench about 4" to 6" (10cm to 15cm) deep in front of the rail, up to a distance of about half the height of the fence in front. Stand a row of boards, which must be at least 1.5" (40mm) thick in the trench; check them for uprightness and nail them to the top rail. On reasonably gentle slopes a spirit level can be used to make sure that the boards are upright. On steeper slopes they may look odd if they are dead upright, so use your eye and judgement to make them look aesthetically correct.

Cut off the tops of the palisade timbers, ideally at an angle

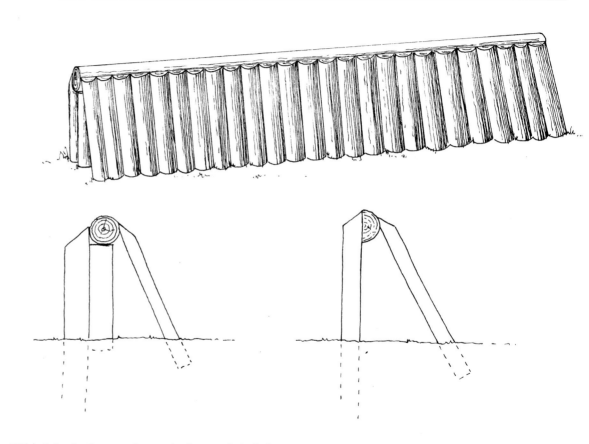

20(a). Palisade. Construction method one: rails built first.

sloping downwards, using the top rail as a guide (assuming it is straight enough) then rasp the edges to make them less sharp. Be careful not to catch the nails with the saw; to prevent this happening they should be put in as low down the frame rail as possible.

The problem with this method of constructing a palisade is that if the fence looks wrong when completed, altering it will be very awkward. It is often difficult to assess what height it should be until you see it with all the boards attached. An alternative method, if you have a tractor and loader or forklift with enough lift, is to build the whole fence flat then move it into position in one piece. Use half-round rails as a frame – one at the top and one at half its height. Nail the palisade timbers to the flat sides of the frame half-rounds, and cut the excess off along the top one. Pick up the whole structure with a chain round the top rail so that it hangs down balanced. To achieve this it may be necessary to remove one board from the centre. Lean the structure against posts that have already been put in the right place. The fence can now be looked at and measured, the angle of lean adjusted, and the height corrected by altering the amount of timber in the ground or by cutting off the bottom of the boards. It can be left like this until the course has been inspected. Then the rails can be roped to the posts.

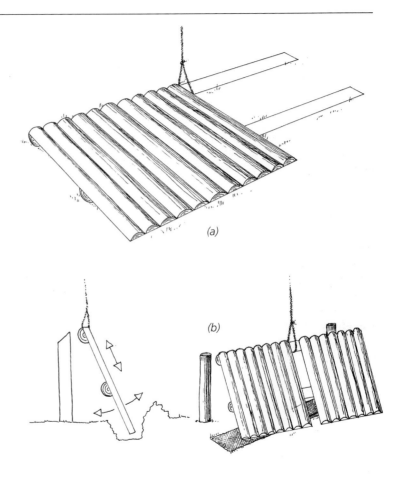

*20(a). Palisade. Construction method two: structure built flat (a).*
*then offered-up to posts (b).*

A **seat** or **park-type bench** can be built on a post and rail framework. Build a plain set of rails and then an approximately half-height set about 2' to 4' (60cm-120cm) out in front. The back section will need a lower rail, level with or slightly lower than the front rail. Fill the space between these two poles with boards no less than 1.5" (40mm) thick. They may have gaps between them but, once again, they must not be big enough for a horse's foot to go through. Cut the boards off behind the line of the front of the pole and angle them back to make them less sharp if a horse should hit them, but before doing so make sure that the nails are well out of the way. As an alternative, use a half-round rail for the front

*21(a). Seat or park bench.*

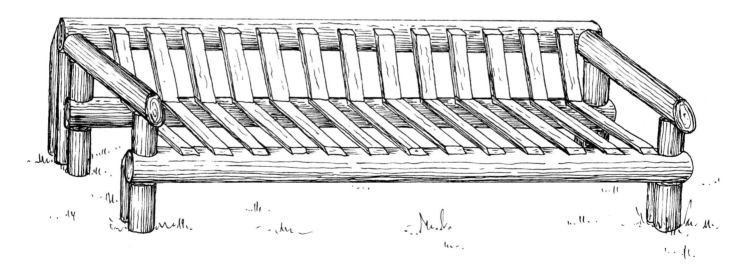

and fix a secure batten to the back of it. Nail the boards to the batten so that they are flush with the top of the rail. Fix similar battens onto the top of the horizontal boards and below and slightly in front of the top rail. Nail more boards to the batten and to the top rail, to form the back of the seat. Cut them off along the top of the top rail, angled downwards as with the palisade, and rasp the edges.

If the outside front posts are left protruding, spare pieces of timber can be fixed from them to the outside back posts, to form arms. Any cut edges should be rounded and rasped, for safety.

If correctly proportioned and solidly built, a seat is an inviting fence to jump.

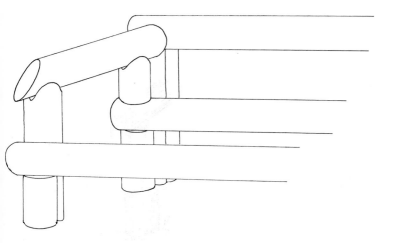

*21(b). Frame before slats are fitted.*

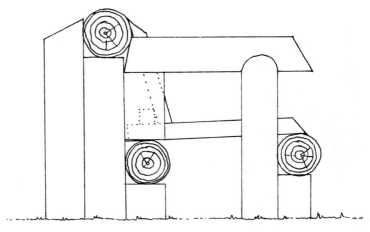

*21(c). Side view.*

22(a). Pheasant feeder; single
pitch roof.

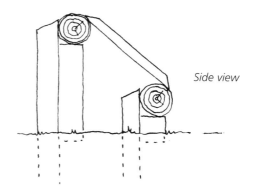

Side view

A **pheasant feeder** or **lamb creep** consists of two or three rails with a roof between them. Round or half-rounds can be used for the frame. The feeder can have a single or double pitch roof: the single one being the easier to construct. Be careful not to make the base-spread too wide. The lower rails should be about half, or slightly less than half, the height of the top ones. Sawmill offcuts can be used for the roof, but they must be strong enough – at least 1.5" (40mm) thick; otherwise, extra frame timbers may be needed. Alternatively, boards or half-rounds can be used, as with the palisade. At the leading edge, the cladding must be cut off behind the line of the pole, angled backwards, and rasped to remove the sharp edges.

22(b). *Pheasant feeder with double pitch roof.*

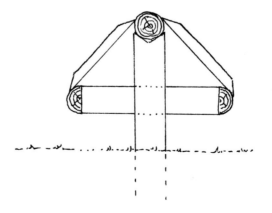

*Side view showing only one row of posts.*

An **elephant trap** is another type of post and rail. It is basically half a **tiger-trap** which is a fence traditionally built over a ditch so that it can be jumped from both sides. Elephant traps are safer for competitions as they only jump one way. The posts are a long way out of the ground and angled steeply, so they must be very firmly anchored. Most post drivers and augers will not work at such a steep angle, so the post holes have to be dug either by hand or with a back-hoe digger. There should be at least as much of the post in the ground as out of it.

The soil should be very firmly compacted back into the hole and on top of the posts, as considerable leverage is exerted if a horse's weight is on the top rail. To make the job easier, hire a jack hammer with a rammer foot on it; it will take the backbreak out of compacting the soil down firm.

It is very difficult to judge the angle at which to put the post in. If possible, offer up the top rail in position by holding it with a forklift or tractor. Even better, have two tractors – one at each end – so that your view of the fence is not obstructed. Make sure that the hydraulic arms don't sink down (as many do) – by propping them with a piece of

*23(a). Elephant trap.*

timber. The posts can then be fitted under the rail, roped on, and the angle adjusted before the hole is filled in. Fit a second rail tight on to the top of the bank of the ditch, to define the take-off, so that there is no danger of a horse's leg sliding underneath it; and a third rail spaced on blocks between the other two.

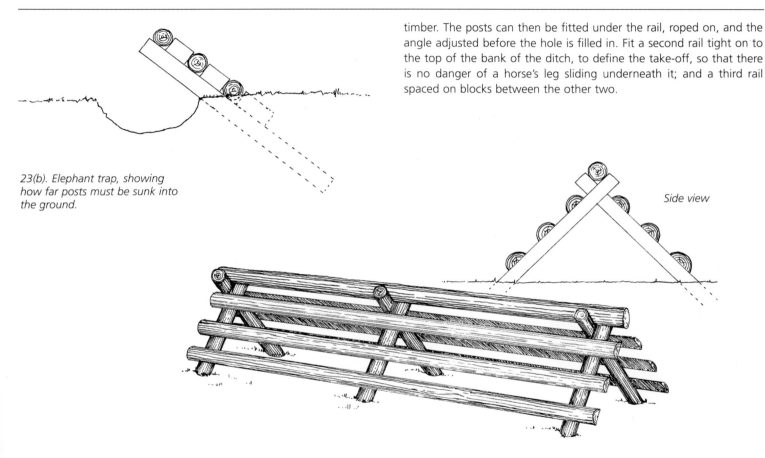

*23(b). Elephant trap, showing how far posts must be sunk into the ground.*

*Side view*

*24. Tiger trap*

Side view

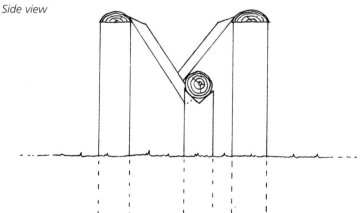

*25. Hay rack, showing the fence before the groundline (pole or straw bales) has been put in place.*

A **hayrack** consists of parallel rails with slats at the centre. Built incorrectly this is a potentially dangerous fence as not only may it have a false ground line, but extracting a cast horse from it would be very difficult. To make it safe it must have a lower rail on the front of the posts or, better still, the front should be filled in with bales to bring the ground line out in front. The slats must be strong enough and close enough together to support a horse's weight or, preferably they should be covered with bales which are boarded over.

# 2 Jointed and Curved Rails

When building more complex fences it may be necessary to join two rails together to make a longer run, or to construct a curved set of rails, either concave or convex, or through a depression in the ground, or over a bump. The easiest curved and jointed fence to build is convex: i.e. curved at its centre towards the horse as he approaches. Try to match the sizes of the rails where they join by using the same long piece of timber and cutting it where the joins have to be made. If the piece runs out, join the poles big end to big end or small end to small end – remembering to have the big ends downhill wherever possible. Where the poles meet at the posts, cut them together. The ideal angle at which to cut is the bisector of the angle of the poles: then if the poles are the same diameter both joint cuts should match.

To tidy the joint, continue to run the bar of the chainsaw through the cut, pushing the poles together after each cut until they are a good fit. Make sure that the poles are long enough in the first place to allow for this extra cutting. Both rails sit on the same dummy post and because of the angle, they will have a good bearing on the post. However, if the rails are joined in a straight line or concave curve this method does not work. The rails only bear on the very middle of the post, and if they are hit hard they can easily slip past it, so some carpentry with the chainsaw will be required.

Choose rails with matching diameters, as before. If the ground is sloping, start at the downhill end. Lay the first pole on the dummy where the joint is to be made so that it is level with the outside of the post, and rope it to the post at its other end. Slice down to half the

depth of the pole so that it is level with the other side of the post. Then cut it horizontally from the end, back to the bottom of the cut, and remove the half-round block which it forms. Lay the next pole on top of the cut, prop it on a jack or high dummy at the other end, and rope it on. Place it so that it is a saw bar's width away from your vertical cut on the other pole. Now slice upwards half its depth, level with the end of the other pole. Take it down and cut out the bottom half-round chock. It should now fit reasonably on to the cut made in the first pole. The joint can be tidied by running the bar through the cuts as before. *Note: Be extremely careful. Pushing the bar of the saw into a cut is the most dangerous operation that can be carried out – because when the tip of the bar touches the timber there is a great risk of it kicking back. Use a saw with a nose wheel on the bar; keep it very sharp, with the chain properly tight; and run the*

26. Joining rails. (a). Rails half overlapped.

26. *Joining rails. (b). Roped.*

engine at full revs before pushing the bar in. *Make sure that you are wearing the correct safety clothing and that your assistants are well out of the way.* In the case of concave joints the technique can be further refined by making the vertical cuts at an angle from the outside of the post at the back to the middle of the joint at the front, so that the joint will be almost invisible. Practise these techniques on some scrap timber before attempting them and risking wasting good materials. The alternative is to put two posts in for each join so that each end of each rail has sufficient support. This is probably best for rails which go through dips or over bumps in the ground.

## Brush Fences

The most common and attractive brush fences are naturally-growing hedges, but they are seldom suitable to be jumped in their natural state and will require reinforcement with timber. Even if they have been kept trimmed, most hedges will be too big to jump. Just cutting them down may result in a line of large stumps, which are unsafe. The best option is to cut and lay the hedge: an ages-old operation carried out to keep hedgerows in good condition as well as stockproof. During winter the stems of the hedge are cut almost through and are then laid (bent forwards) all in the same direction. They are kept in position by stakes with binders which are intertwined along the top of the stakes. The now horizontal stems grow new shoots which fill the hedge out from the ground upwards. When this operation has been carried out it is important to keep sheep and other livestock away, with wire netting, as they will eat the new shoots and ruin the hedge.

After a couple of years, if the cut and laid hedge is kept trimmed and looked after it will take on an attractive leafy appearance but, even with its stakes and binders, it will not stand up to competition use. It only takes one horse to hit it hard and a hole will be made which will be almost impossible to repair quickly. A post and rail fence will therefore have to be built into the hedge to reinforce it: which can be difficult, as the rails must be clearly visible to the horse but not too far out in front of the hedge, giving the fence a false ground line.

If possible, put the posts in behind the hedge, with the rail on top of the binders; to make this easier you may be able to push the posts into the back of the hedge, which is best done with a mechanical post driver. (Digging post holes successfully in a hedge is almost impossible.) If solid timber is hidden out of sight in a fence, a horse may think that

*b*

*c*

*27. Cut and laid hedges. (a).Continuously growing hedge with stems part cut through and laid horizontally; (b). and (c).,created from one large thorn bush.*

he can brush through it, resulting in a very nasty fall. Ideally the hedge should spread out underneath the rail so that a lower rail may not be needed, but the hedge may take a couple of years to mature. Meanwhile you should fill underneath the rail with fir branches to give the fence an ascending shape. Be sure to remove the branches after the competition as they will prevent the hedge from growing naturally.

Most rules allow the part of an obstacle which a horse can brush through to be up to 6" (150mm) higher than the solid part. Keep the hedge trimmed at this height, with the rail clearly visible, and you will have an attractive and inviting fence for many years to come.

61

**Oxer Rails**. Before barbed wire was invented, farmers built post and rail fences to prevent cattle from damaging their hedges. They were known as oxer rails ( from oxa, the Old English for ox). In some cases a rail was built on each side of a hedge to prevent cattle touching noses (health hazard). A hedge with a rail on one side is called a 'single oxer' and a hedge with a rail on both sides is called a 'double oxer'. A double oxer is basically a parallel rails with a hedge in the middle. Sometimes a parallel without a hedge is called an oxer.

*27(d). Double oxer.*

**Artificial Brush Fences.** When no natural hedges are available, brush fences can be made by using a frame stuffed with birch twigs or fir branches. To make the frame, first put up a row of posts as for a post and rail fence (installing all the posts, not just the end ones). Cut the tops of the middle posts into a wedge shape: i.e. an upturned 'V' when looked at from the front. This prevents too big a gap forming in the brush above the posts.

Attach half-round rails to the posts with wire or studding (threaded rod) and nuts and washers, counter-sinking the nuts on the take-off side. The strongest rail should be at top front. The top back one should not be higher than the top front. Then nail another pair of half-round rails on either side of the posts on the ground.

The rails of a brush frame need not be as high as those of a plain rail fence as the brush has to be jumped as well. The lower the rails the more flexible the brush will be and the easier it will be for the horse to push through it. (Rails should be 10"/250mm below the top of the brush.) The frame should be wide enough for whole bundles of birch to be packed into it; if it isn't, the bundles will have to be cut and made smaller. If the birch is more than 18" (45cm) longer than necessary, trim the bottoms off the bundles: the top of the fence will then have the flexible twigs in it rather than the solid sticks.

Arrange about three of four bundles in the frame and then compress them tight: a winch is the best tool for this. Put the cable round the bundles and back onto the winch or to the end post of the fence.

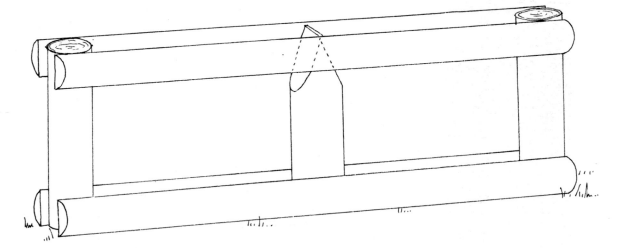

28. Building a birch fence.
(a). The frame.

b

c

Pull it in steadily: it is surprising how much the birch will compress. If you do not have a winch, use a rope and tractor or other vehicle, but be careful not to spin the wheels and make marks on the ground. You will need a driver and a helper to give directions. Use a crow bar to tap the birch to encourage it to pull up straight. Leave the rope anchored tight and push in another 3 to 4 bundles; put the rope round them, and pull again. Keep doing this until the whole section of the frame is full. To fill the last little bit of a section it may be necessary to cut a couple of bundles and put the birch in, one twig at a time. After a section is filled, it should be so firm that there is no way in which a horse could trap his leg inside the frame. This is a vital safety point. The birch can be further arranged by tapping it with a bar or sledge hammer.

When you have filled in all the sections of the fence, it is time to cut off the top. To do this you will need, preferably, a petrol-driven hedge-trimmer: or if you have the patience, a very good pair of garden shears. You can cut the birch with a chainsaw, but it is dangerous and tends to smash the ends of the twigs. To do the job tidily and at the right height you will need some form of guide-line to run the cutter bar along – such as a sawn fencing rail which can be tacked or screwed to stakes attached to the frame of the fence. Position this at the required height with a measuring stick. Then run the hedge-cutter along it. Cutting compressed birch will be hard work even for a good quality petrol cutter, especially if there are a lot of big twigs in the section that is being cut. Take time, and do not overload the machine. When the excess has been cleared, trim the front and back to remove any protruding twigs. Check the height, and adjust it if necessary.

*28. Building a birch fence. (b). The frame prepared for stuffing; (c). the first few bundles of birch being compressed.*

Sometimes an uneven cut can be adjusted by tapping the top of the birch with the back of a spade; and the top can be made less stiff by cutting it at an angle higher at the back than the front. To give it aesthetic appeal, leave a small turret of birch at either end of the fence.

A similar fence can be made by the same technique, using fir branches such as spruce. These cannot be bundled, so will have to be stuffed in to the frame one branch at a time. They provide a less stiff brush fence than birch, and the needles although green to begin with, will soon wither, go brown, and need replacing.

Brush fences look better with an apron built on the front (which can simply be greenery laid over straw bales) with a half-round rail to act as a take-off pole and to contain the bales. Do not fit the rail until the

28. Building a birch fence. (d). Cutting to size.

29. Birch apron. (a). Horizontal birch bundles about to be wired over a stepped bale base.

bales are in place, so that it can be an equal number of bale widths away from the front of the fence. As with rail fences, do not have too big a base-spread: no more than the height of the fence.

To make a birch apron, first attach wires to the inside of the take-off rail at about 3' (1m) intervals. An easy way of doing this is to use 'gripples' – small fencing-wire joiners which slide over the wire one way but will not slide off the other. Knock a staple almost home into the rail and pass the wire through it. Then slide a gripple onto the end of the wire; it will be locked firm. The wires should be long enough to reach over the apron and through the back of the fence, with a bit to spare.

Stack the bales in a step formation, then lay the bundles of birch horizontally over them. So that the fence will look tidy, put the twiggy or small ends of the bundles on the outsides, with the butt ends meeting in the middle. You will need to open a few bundles and feed in the individual twigs, alternate ways round, to cover over the ugly woody ends. When this is done, pass the wires over the birch and through the back of the fence under the top rails. If the back has been properly stuffed you will need some form of 'needle' to thread the wire through – such as a 2' (60cm) length of ½" (12mm) steel rod with a hole in one end and a loop or handle on the other. Push the rod through the brush from the back. Thread the wire through the hole and bend it double. Then pull the wire, through the fence. Knock a staple into the bottom of the back rail; pass the wire through the staple and slide a gripple onto it (using fencing pliers or the tool sold with gripples); pull the wire and the gripple will lock it tight. If using fencing pliers, be careful that they do not slip, because if they do you are likely to bash yourself on the nose. Make sure that the tension is equal on all the wires. The apron should now be solid enough for man or horse to jump on it

without damaging it. Trim off all the 'whiskers', fold the outside lengths of birch down over the ends of the bales (to hide them) and secure them with another wire. Note that this type of apron should be built only a few days before a competition and cleared away soon afterwards, as the bales will go soft if they are rained on, and will make the fence unsafe.

Alternatively, the bales can be covered with fir branches, which do not need to be wired if the ends of the stems are poked into the bales, or if the front bales are stood on their ends so that the strings are at the front and the branches can be woven in and out of the them. As this type of apron may become damaged if a horse banks the fence, it is necessary to brief the fence judge to tidy it up from time to time.

A fir-branch apron can be built in front of a timber fence, with no brush on top of it, to make an inviting fence for an early part of a course or after several difficult fences. The gap under the top rail must be filled-in in such a way that the bales cannot be pushed out of the back of the fence by a refusing horse. Again, these aprons are only temporary and should be built and cleared away just before and after the competition.

A genuine steeplechase fence is a slightly more complex construction than that described above. For horse trials these are usually portable, so that they can be moved from site to site.

29. *Birch apron. (b). The trimmed and completed fence.*

## Other Plain Fences

The following are some other plain fences that are commonly found on most cross-country courses.

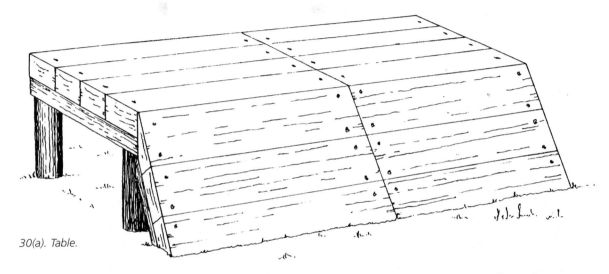

30(a). Table.

A **table** is usually made out of railway sleepers/railroad ties. Tables went out of fashion in the UK after one or two accidents to riders who had fallen at them. However, when built and sited in the correct way they do jump satisfactorily. When using sleepers the fence must be at least two sleepers wide.

Put in two rows of three posts at slightly less distances apart than the desired spread for the fence. Estimate the maximum eventual height and cut off the posts two sleeper thicknesses lower. Lay bearers, made from short sleepers, across each pair of posts, then put sleepers on top of these: two at the front and two at the back. Check the height measurement again, and have a good look at the fence. If the height is OK, cut a further 2" (50mm) off the front posts. This will give a slope to the top of the table, which ensures that the horse can see the spread. Fix the bearers down with wire or pins.

Lay the deck sleepers on the bearers, starting from the front. You will find that they are not all the same size and shape and that they will need juggling with to make them fit tidily. They can be fixed down with 8" (200mm) nails or pins. When a suitable fit has been achieved, cut off the remaining bearer that is sticking out at the back.

The in-filling of the front is the most important safety feature. It is advisable to in-fill the whole way to the ground, with the bottom sloping out in front. This is because, when looked at from the front, the top sleepers give a comparatively thin profile, compared with a large round pole – thus making it less easy for a horse to judge where to take off. If the front is solid there will be no doubt.

Bolt, or wire, angled struts to the top of the posts. These should come out at least 1' (30cm) in front; check the rules for the base-spread measurement. Stack sleepers on their edges from the ground up to the top, but do not nail them. When the top sleeper is on, remember that it will affect the top spread. You will be very lucky if the front sleepers come flush with the top of the table; they will need adjusting by digging in the bottom sleepers before fixing.

When all is tidy, fix with 8" (200mm) nails or pins. Most sleepers are 5" (125mm) thick, and the nails will go through them. Recently 6" (150mm) sleepers have become available, but they are too thick for nails, so pins must be used.

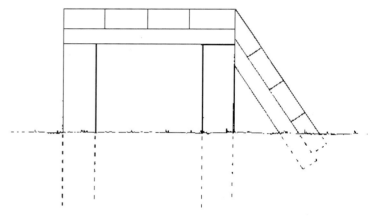

*30(b). Table. Side view, showing the solid sloping front.*

*31. Log Pile.*

A **log pile** is an attractive, inviting and safe fence. Building a solid log pile would entail using a vast amount of timber and would be very wasteful, so most log piles are built hollow in the middle. Getting the height correct is difficult, especially if you are using very uneven timber. The frame should be similar to that for a table.

Ideally the log pile should be rounded on top, which can be achieved by using larger diameter poles, or by making the frame higher, in the middle. Norway Spruce or Red Cedar are probably the best timbers to use as they grow the straightest.

You need to work from top centre downwards. When the maximum height has been set, with the biggest pole at the centre, offer the next one up to it and rotate it with a turning lever to find the position where it fits best to the other pole. You can make it fit more accurately by running the chainsaw down the gap between the two poles, gradually creating a better and better fit. It is more important to make

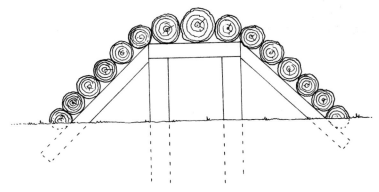

*Side view, showing thickest pole at centre to create a rounded cap.*

71

the poles on the front and back a good fit, than it is for those on the top, as they cannot be seen so well.

Once in position, the poles can be fixed with pins, bolts or wire. When you progress to the front and back, use a pair of jacks to raise each pole up to the one above and to tighten them together as they are cut. At ground level it may be necessary to dig quite a bit out to help you get the bottom pole in. The open ends can be stacked with off-cuts to improve the log pile illusion.

This type of fence can also be built with half-rounds, which is cheaper and a little easier – the drawback being that the ends do not look so good.

A **cordwood stack** is a log pile with the logs the other way on – their cut ends facing the horse as it approaches. It is a very difficult fence to build satisfactorily, as it requires a lot of timber in a variety of diameters. The bulk of it can be made of scrap timber from redundant fences, as long as it is not too rotten.

*32(a). Cordwood stack.*

A frame will be needed to give the fence strength and to define its height and spread. It is basically a parallel rails with no centre posts and no lower rails.

Stack your largest timbers under the rails so that they come out in front about 1' (30cm) 2' (60cm) to give the fence an ascending shape. The next layer above these should be slightly shorter and should have the back vertically over those underneath, creating a step-shape at the front. Keep working like this until the bottom of the rails is reached.

The tricky part is working out the sizes of timber so that they will fit neatly underneath the top rail. When this has been achieved, fill in the gap between the two top rails with lengths of timber so that they are no higher than the back rail. Chamfer off any sharp edges where the logs stick out in front of the fence. Then rake up and clear away all the bark and sawdust.

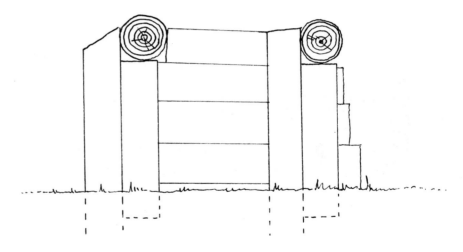

32(b). Cordwood stack: side view showing basic parallel frame with logs below protruding to give good groundline.

An ordinary **wooden five-bar gate** can be used to make a fence. In their natural state these are not strong enough and need re-reinforcing. The easiest method is to build a post and rail fence, lean the gate up against it, and rope it on. A gate will always jump better if it is leaning away from the horse to create the ascending shape that jumps best. This is not very natural looking for a gate, which is a very upright structure – but you should never sacrifice the safe jumpability of a fence in favour of its appearance. Instead of leaning the gate up against a post and rail fence, you could attach a piece of 2" x ¼" (50mm x 6mm) flat steel with coach bolts to the back of the top rail and then lean the gate against two sawn posts like normal gate posts. Alternatively, you can have an upright gate with a ground rail or pole sited in front of it.

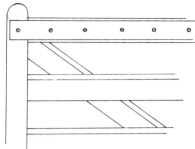

*(b). Steel reinforcement with coach bolts.*

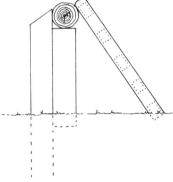

*(c). Side view showing the gate.*

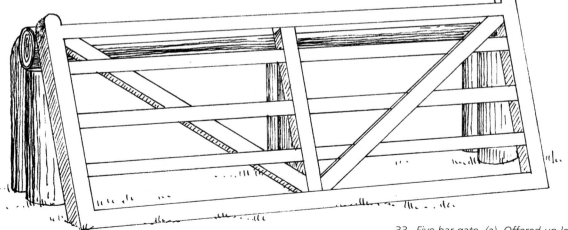

*33. Five bar gate. (a). Offered-up leaning, before being roped.*

**Tyres** are not as popular as they used to be, and are not very attractive to look at, but fixed in the right way they can make very safe and forgiving obstacles – especially for schooling. Car tyres are a bit too small for most applications, which is a pity, as they are plentiful, and many tyre dealers are glad to give them away. Lorry tyres are the most useful size but unfortunately these days most of them are sent for re-treading and are not available cheaply.

To use tyres for a fence, arrange them in stacks of equal dimensions; the sizes are stamped on them: most of the internal diameters are in imperial inches. The outside dimensions of cross-ply tyres are in imperial, and those of radials are in millimetres.

You will need two strong, straight, not too large poles to thread through the tyres; scaffold tubes are ideal for this. Slide the tyres over the poles, with the smallest ones in the middle and the largest at the outside edges. Then manoeuvre the whole arrangement up to a pair of posts and fix it – the poles should be forced apart with blocks to keep the tyres tight.

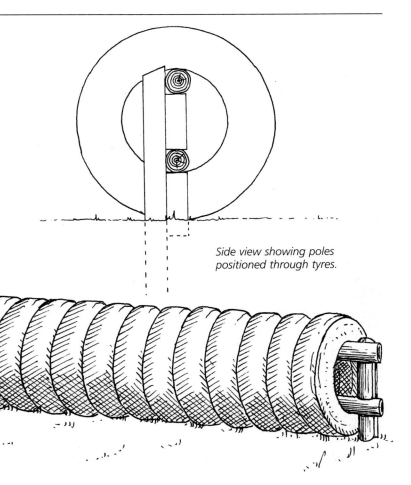

*Side view showing poles positioned through tyres.*

34. *Tyres, supported by posts and centre poles.*

75

**Walls** are sometimes natural features on a course site. Most are of the dry stone variety; are generally not strong enough to be jumped without reinforcement; and often have sharp coping stones on top which could hurt a horse.

A natural dry stone wall in good condition may be reinforced quite simply by driving stout fencing stakes down the back and front. It is often impossible to position the stakes right up against the base of the wall, as the foundations spread wider, but get them as close as you can.

Take off all the coping stones, to achieve the right height, and replace them with railway sleepers, which should be firmly attached to the stakes with wire or bolts. This should protect the wall from the horses and the horses from the wall.

A dry stone wall can also be built from scratch. Make a frame from a row of stout pressure-treated posts and build the wall round them. Cap the wall with timber fixed to the top of the posts. A machined half-round rail on the leading edge will make a safe and smart finish to the job.

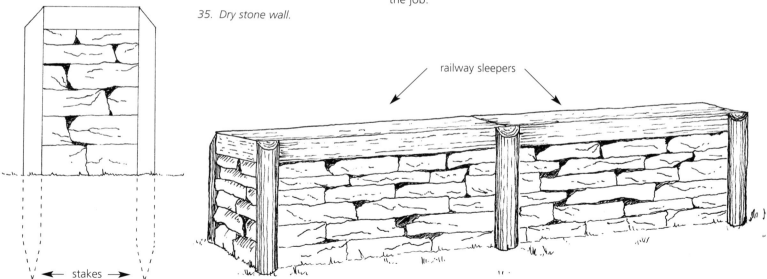

*35. Dry stone wall.*

railway sleepers

← stakes →

A **concrete breeze-block wall** is not difficult to construct and is easy to cap off safely. This type of wall will need a good concrete footing in a trench dug into the ground. When concreting the trench think about the eventual height of the wall, so that you can be sure to use an even number of courses of blocks. Use the largest size of hollow block available.

Start building at each end, then run a string line from end to end to keep the intermediate blocks level and straight. Each time a new course is started, use a spirit level at each end to keep the whole wall upright. For the mortar, use about three or four parts sand to one part cement and mix it until it has a plastic texture. When the top course of blocks is on, embed in mortar lengths of ½" (12mm) studding, with their bottom ends bent double, into the hollows of the blocks and leave them until the mortar has hardened. Offer sleepers or large half-rounds on top of the studding, and mark where they will go. Drill holes in the timber and make countersink holes on the upper sides. Slide the timber over the studding and tighten it down into the countersinks with nuts and washers. Cut off the excess studding, flush with the top of the timber. Leave it for at least a fortnight so that the mortar will harden fully before the fence is jumped for the first time.

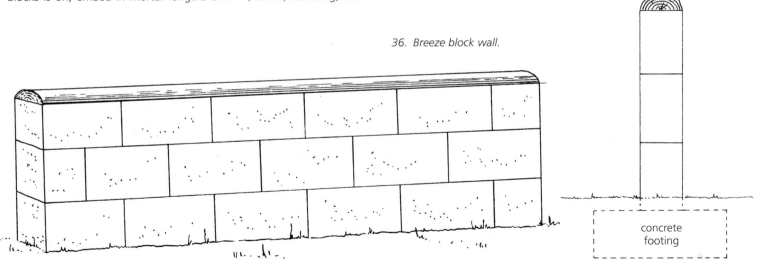

36. *Breeze block wall.*

concrete
footing

# 5 Ground Work

When building a new course, the ground work should be carried out first, to give the newly disturbed earth and hard-core as much time as possible to settle. A course-builder can pay heavily for mistakes made with ground work, and it is usually very difficult, if not impossible, to correct mistakes in the middle of a competition. So be sure to bear this in mind, and take no shortcuts.

37. Sloping sided ditch with take-off pole.

## Ditches

Unless a ditch is fairly shallow, has gently sloping sides covered with well-established vegetation, and is only going to be used for a very few horses in dry weather, it will need some form of timber work to reinforce the take-off edge. This is known as 'revetting'. The most basic form of revetting is a take-off pole, which is only suitable for sloping sided ditches where there is to be light use. Only pressure-treated timber is suitable for use on or below the ground.

A telegraph pole is the ideal take-off rail. Lay it on the ground at the edge of the ditch so that it is firmly on land and not in the ditch itself. There must be sound earth at the back of the pole.

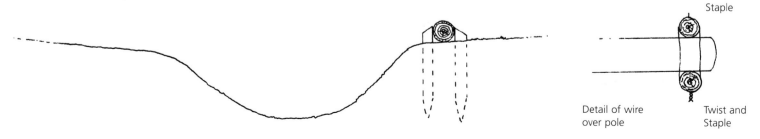

Staple

Detail of wire over pole

Twist and Staple

If you are digging a ditch, the width of the take-off rail must be included in the spread measurement. Cut along both sides of the pole with a spade, then roll the pole out of the way. Dig out about one-third to one-half the depth of the pole's thickness. Roll the pole back and check it for fit. If necessary take it out again and adjust it. Drive pairs of pressure treated half-round stakes into each side of the pole: three pairs to an 18' (5.5m) pole. Wire the stakes together securely with wire and staples. Tighten the wire by tapping the stakes further into the ground, but don't overdo this as it will eventually loosen the stakes again.

Cut the stake tops off at an angle sloping down and away from the pole, then rasp the cut edges. The pole must be fitted in such a way that after the ground has become worn there is no possibility of a horse's leg slipping under the pole into the ditch.

All other ditches will need properly revetting right down to the bottom. If a ditch has a fence over it, only revet the take-off side. The traditional way of doing this is with railway sleepers/railroad ties. First, the side of the ditch must be cut down vertically. (Remember to include the revetting timbers within the measurement for the spread of the obstacle). The top sleeper should be flush with the top of the ditch – so to achieve this dig down an equal number of sleeper widths. As all sleepers are not the same length, it is as well to measure them all at the start of the job and to chalk their lengths on them, so that you can pair them up to keep the works even.

Lay the bottom sleepers on the the prepared shelf that has been dug. Drive half-round pressure-treated stakes at least 18" (45cm) into the bottom of the ditch. There should be one stake at the outside ends of the sleepers and one over the join between the two. Tie a string line to the two outside stakes to keep the others in line – otherwise they will not all touch the sleepers. Now lay a second layer of sleepers, like bricks, on top of the first. Cut one sleeper in half and put the two halves at the outside ends and a full sleeper in the middle. Drive in a

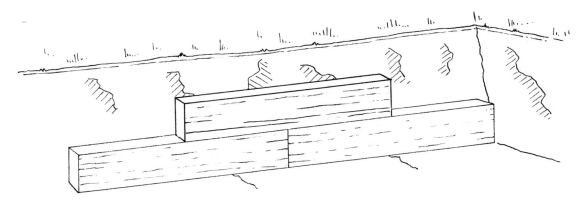

38. *Revetting with sleepers.(a).*
*Bottom two sleepers levelled,*
*with first sleeper of second row in*
*position.*

79

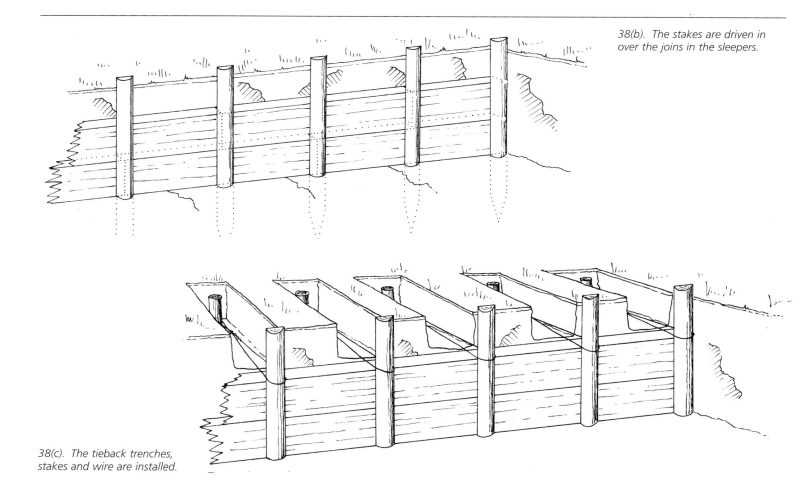

38(b). The stakes are driven in over the joins in the sleepers.

38(c). The tieback trenches, stakes and wire are installed.

further two half-round stakes over the joins between the sleepers. It is best not to fix the sleepers to the stakes until all the layers are on, so that you can allow for height adjustment.

When all the sleepers are on and the top height has been judged to be OK, nail through the stakes into all but the top sleepers with 5" (125mm) or 6" (150mm) nails. Angle the nails, to make them less likely to pull out. Take the top sleepers off again and move them out of the way.

The stakes into the bottom of the trench are not strong enough to hold up the sleepers and the weight of material behind them: they only anchor the bottom of the revetment. The structure must be tied back into the bank with wire: use nothing less than No.8 gauge (4mm) soft wire.

Dig a trench a spade wide, a spade deep, and at least 1' (30cm) more than the height of the sleepers in the bank opposite each stake. At the end of this trench, drive in at least 18" (45cm) a pressure-treated stake at an angle leaning back away from the ditch. Pass a loop of wire round the stake which is holding the sleepers. Bring the two ends round the back of the trench-stake and twist them together on the front of it, or cross them and staple them down firmly. When this has been done for all the stakes, tighten the wires by twisting them up with a short bar. They should all be brought up to the same tension, but be careful not to overtighten them and pull the revetment over. Refit the top sleepers, and nail them. If the ends of the sleepers are away from the bank, you will need short pieces of sleeper to close the gap. Dig these into the bank and wire them to the ends of the other sleepers. If any of them are longer than 3' (1m). drive in a stake and wire it back into the middle of the construction. Cut off the tops of the stakes at an angle sloping down into the ditch, and rasp the cut edges.

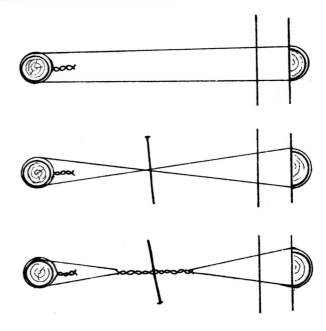

*38(d). View from above of No.8 gauge 4mm soft wire, twisted to tighten.*

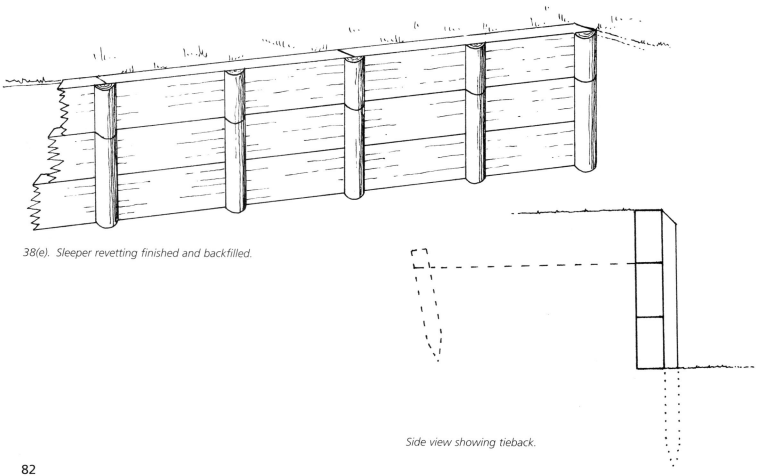

*38(e). Sleeper revetting finished and backfilled.*

*Side view showing tieback.*

**Back filling.** The gap between the sleepers and the bank should be filled in with hard-core and topped with ³/₄" (20mm) crushed stone. Hardcore should always be used, never soil, which takes a very long time to settle, and as horses will sink a long way into it – particularly if it is wet – it is obviously very dangerous.

To fill the greater part of the space any hard-core can be used – such as brick rubble or large road stone. Do not tip big chunks onto the wires as they will tend to stretch them and make them ineffectual. Build up lumps (at first by hand) round the wires, to protect them. Fill with this material to just above the bottom of the top sleeper and then compact it well with a hand-rammer or a rammer-foot on a jack-hammer. Top up to the top of the sleepers with the ³/₄" (20mm) stone and compact it with a vibrating compactor-plate or vibrating roller. If a tracked digger is being used this can compact the material, but keep it away from the edge of the sleepers – as when turned it could move them.

Spread the small stone over the grass beyond the edge of the bank so as not to have a straight, defined line between grass and stone, which to a horse could look like a take-off line. The grass will soon grow through the stone. Grass seed can also be sown onto the stone and, given the right weather conditions, quite a lot of it will grow. A thin layer of top soil – no more than 2" (50mm) may be spread on the stone and seed sown into it. You must then wait until the grass is well established before using the fence. Another option is to lay turf onto the stone. Though it is more expensive, it will establish more quickly than seed.

To narrow down a ditch that is too wide, use the above technique. Measure from the landing side (where a horse can reasonably be expected to land safely) back into the ditch. Build the revetment so that the sleepers are within the maximum distance allowed for a spread (see the rules). If the ditch is very deep it may be best for safety's sake to pipe it to reduce the depth. Should you do this make sure that the pipe is capable of carrying the maximum amount of water which flows along the ditch in winter. For Pony Club courses, a ditch must be at least 18" (45cm) deep, inclusive of the guard rail. If a guard rail is not used, the ditch should be revetted on the take-off side. Do not make the ditch too shallow, or horses may not realise what it is and put their feet in it. If the revetment is some distance from the original bank, particular attention must be made to the sides going at right angles to the bank in order to make sure that they are as strong as the rest of the structure.

## Steps, Drops and Banks

These should be revetted in exactly the same way as ditches: but where considerable height is involved – as in big drops – much more substantial uprights will be needed, such as vertical sleepers; and the wires will need to go much further back into the bank.

Building a flight of steps requires a rudimentary survey – to establish (a) where to start constructing the top and bottom steps, and (b) the suitable depth of each step within the total height available. Steps are normally 9' (2.8m) or 18' (5.5m) apart for jumping either up or down. To make them easier to negotiate it is possible to have a slope of up to 1' (30cm) between the bottom of one step and the top of the next – which is preferable to making them too high. The sides of the steps will need to be revetted in the same way as the narrowed-down ditch (see above paragraph). Some of the sides will serve to keep material in and some to keep it out. Be sure to fill the steps in as you build them – otherwise you may find yourself with a middle step which cannot be reached by anything mechanical.

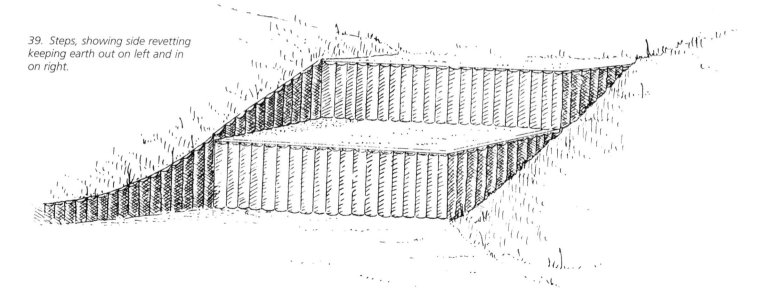

*39. Steps, showing side revetting keeping earth out on left and in on right.*

Banks are built in exactly the same way, but if they are quite small the wires can go across from one side to the other rather than onto stakes in the ground. The weakest parts of a bank are the corners, so it is advisable to fix a diagonal wire between the first stakes in from each side of the corners.

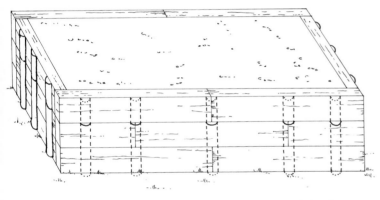

*40. Basic bank constructed from 2 sleepers x 1 sleeper with hardcore fill topped with ¾" (20mm) crushed stone.*

## An Alternative Method of Revetting

In the UK in recent years sleepers have become extremely expensive. Also they are over-engineered for the job; are heavy and awkward to transport and handle – particularly as you are often sliding in and out of a wet and muddy ditch with them; and while stacking them you are liable to pinch your fingers.

There is, however, now another way of doing the same job with materials which are cheaper, lighter, easier to handle and fix, as well as being readily available from most fencing suppliers.

For the horizontals 8' x 3" x 3" (2.4m x 75mm x 75mm) pressure-treated timbers known as '3x3s'are used. These are posts for garden larch-lap panel fencing so are very easy to find; many garden centres stock them. The verticals are 12' x 4" (3.6m x 100mm) pressure-treated, machined half-round rails, commonly used for agricultural fencing.

The ground should be prepared in the same way as for sleepers. Starting at one end, drive a stake made out of a length of half-round into the ground or ditch bottom, as for the sleepers. A scrap piece of timber should also be driven in at the other end. Then stretch tight a string line  between the two stakes at the required height of the revetting. Nail a 3x3 to the first half-round stake, with its top edge along the string. Drive a temporary stake in and screw it to the other end of this timber, preferably with an electric screwdriver so that it can easily be taken off again. If you are likely to be carrying out this operation regularly it is worth making some clamps to hold the spare ends of the 3x3s – using scaffold tubes, which can be knocked in behind the timber. Attach these to short lengths of tube with scaffold clamps, which are adjustable both up and down and in and out, and which

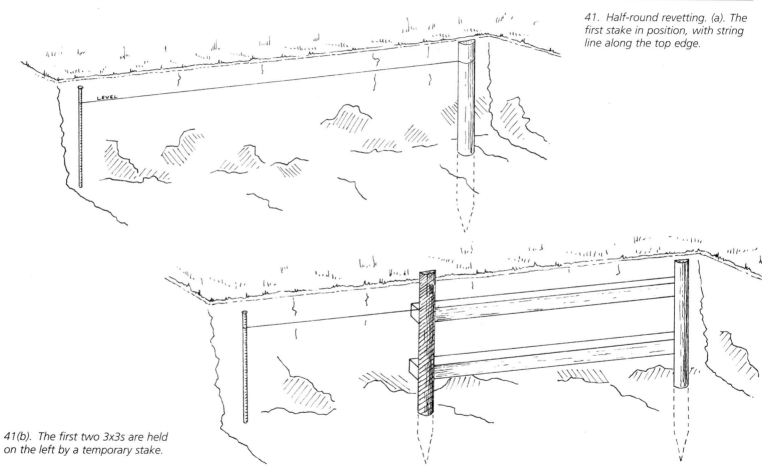

41. Half-round revetting. (a). The first stake in position, with string line along the top edge.

LEVEL

41(b). The first two 3x3s are held on the left by a temporary stake.

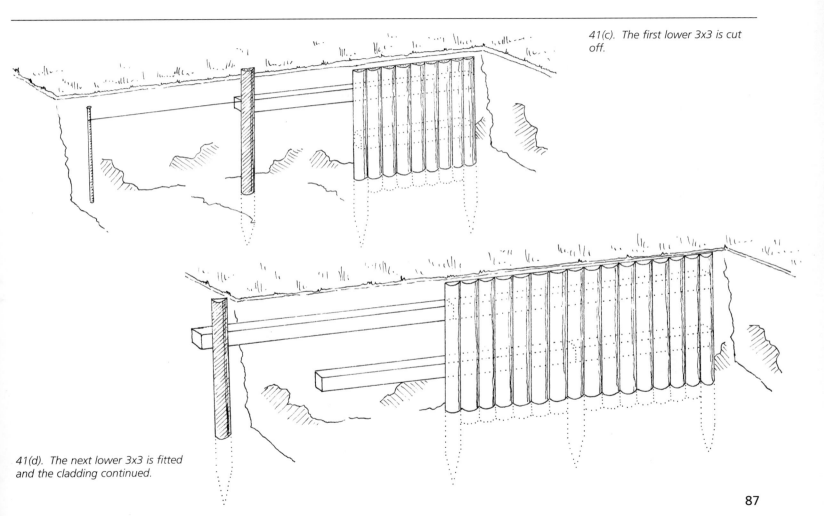

*41(c). The first lower 3x3 is cut off.*

*41(d). The next lower 3x3 is fitted and the cladding continued.*

hold the 3x3s. This structure is much easier to set in the right position than a stake, which can easily go off course.

It is not possible to put a permanent stake in this position at this stage, as the half-rounds are not perfect and never work out to the same dimensions. Fix another 3x3 to the starting stake and the temporary stake (scaffold tube) with a clamp, at half the height of the top one. If the revetment is more than 3'6" (1.1m) high, a third horizontal 3x3 should be used. Make sure that the starting stake is upright in both planes.

Dig a trench about 4" (100m) deep along the base of the 3x3s under the string line, to anchor the bottoms of the verticals. Stand lengths of half-round vertically in the trench and nail them onto the two 3x3s.

*41(e). The whole frame is constructed, with tiebacks installed on the first section.*

Check that each one is vertical with a spirit level before nailing; even though they are machined, they are not perfect and can soon get out of parallel with one another. It is simplest if one person holds the half-round and checks the level while another nails it on, using a compressed-air-powered nail-gun which does the job incredibly quickly.

Keep doing this until you have clad halfway along the first 3x3; it is a good idea to mark the halfway point with chalk before you start, as it is easy to get carried away and go past it. Cut off the bottom 3x3, 2" (5cm) beyond one of the half-rounds. Join another 3x3 to it with skew nails or carpenter's spiked nail plates, and fix it to the temporary

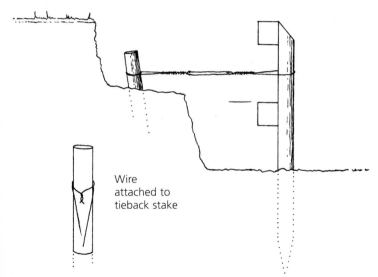

Wire attached to tieback stake

*41(f). Side view showing tieback.*

stake or scaffold tube clamp. Check that its other end is vertically below the string line. Drive in a half-round – which should be at least 1' (30cm) longer than those with which you are cladding – over the join. Nail it on and continue cladding to the end of the top 3x3.

At this stage the temporary stake will have to be removed. As you have two stakes driven in, the work done so far will now stand up on its own. If a clamp has been used on the back it can be left on until it is needed elsewhere. Cut the top 3x3 off 2" (5cm) beyond the last cladding half-round, and knock a longer stake in over the end. Now join another 3x3 on and skew-nail it to the first and the driven-in half-round. Support the other end with a temporary stake or clamp, and carry on the process until the other end is reached. Cut off the tops of the half-rounds along the 3x3 sloping down into the ditch, and rasp the cut edges.

Some people like to fit a half-round along the top of the 3x3 to make a more visible edge for the horse, in which case you should cut the tops off horizontally. Backfill the trench carefully at the bottom and compact both sides of the timbers well, to prevent them from moving. This is particularly important and difficult if it is under water – as is often the case. If necessary, clad-in the sides in exactly the same fashion.

Each of the stakes which is over a join in or at the end of one of the 3x3s, and is driven in, should be wired back, as with the sleepers. Pass the wire around the half-round about 10" (25cm) below the top. Use a battery drill and a ¼" (6mm) bit to make a way for the wire through between the half-rounds, or knock a large nail through and pull it out again. Be careful when tensioning the wire, as it is easier to overtighten and pull the revetting beyond the vertical than with the sleepers. **Caution: *Never use 240-volt power tools when working in water or even in slightly damp conditions.***

This construction method is far more flexible when it comes to revetting awkward shapes than using sleepers. Short 4' (1.2m) sections can be built with a change of angle after each one. Thus a circle or half-circle can be made. Also, the angle can be changed up or down in order to follow undulating ground, in which case the 3x3s are joined between two half-rounds. Cut the 3x3s at an angle, so that the one with the driven-in and wired stake on it is in front of the one without. Over the joins in the 3x3s on their undersides, nail offcuts of half-rounds (or use spiked nail plates) to give extra support to the joins, which are the weakest part of the construction.

You can carry enough of the above-mentioned alternative materials on the back of a pick-up truck to revet most ditches, whereas you would need a trailer to carry enough sleepers for the same job. What is more, when cutting these materials no damage is done to the chainsaw.

42. *Curved half-round revetting. (a). Steps after a ditch and before a circular turret or 'pimple', connected with Weldoning to an alternative palisade on the right.*

*42. Curved half-round revetting. (b). Seen from the top of the steps looking downwards.*

*42. Curved half-round revetting.(c). Close-up of obstacle, looking upwards, with 'pimple' and Weldoning at the top.*

# Water

No two water obstacles are the same. It is always best to construct a water complex where water occurs naturally, rather than making something completely artificial. If you are asked for advice on how to build a water fence in ground which will not hold water, the first thing to say is 'Don't'. It is extremely expensive and complicated: the water could well cost more than all the rest of the fences on a course put together. However, with a big enough budget anything can be done.

Mistakes made when building water obstacles are even more dire and difficult to rectify than those made with other ground work. So, again, no shortcuts with either works or materials. If you cannot afford the time or the money to do the job properly, leave it: the course will be better with no water obstacle than with bad ones!

If horses are expected to jump into the water the current rules require that it should be at least 19'6" (6m) wide, or 29'6" (9m) if there is a step up out. This is to ensure that a bold horse does not attempt to jump from one side to the other and possibly land on the revetting of a step-out and hurt himself very badly.

Only gravel-bottomed running streams and rivers can be used without any sort of modification to the floor, but they will need work on the entrance and exit to make them usable. Any pond or lake must have all the accumulated silt and leaf litter cleared out, and a hard-core base put in its place.

A water obstacle cannot be built with the water in it. It may not be possible to remove water from a running river, but streams can usually be diverted temporarily. Be careful not to fall foul of the local Water Authority if you start playing around with running water, which makes the best type of obstacle, as it tends to stay cleaner, and the sound of splashing helps the horse to know what he is about to jump into.

Water fences which cause horses to fall, extracting from riders the cry 'There's a hole', are those in shade under trees and filled with very muddy-coloured water. A horse's eyesight is not the same as a human's and he hasn't walked the course first, so he only has a split second to make up his mind about what he is seeing. He thinks that flat, still, mud-coloured water is simply earth, and he tries to jump onto rather than into it. It can be likened to coming downstairs in the dark and thinking that you have reached the bottom step when you haven't. Even experienced advanced horses can fall after jumping down an 18" (45cm) step into water, because they react with their legs as though they were going to land on the surface of the water rather than reaching the bottom. (If you threw a handful of pebbles into the water as a horse arrived, to make ripples, he would realise that it was water and would jump in with no difficulty). To overcome such problems, circulate the water continuously with a pump so that it splashes back in like a fountain, making a noise as well as ripples. Be careful to ensure that the water flowing back in does not wash away any of the stone floor.

Before building a water obstacle in a natural pond or lake it is essential to do some basic surveying. Water always lies absolutely level, so if the water is to be the same depth all over the obstacle the floor must also be dead level. It is best to have no more than 6" (150mm) of water, but at this depth if the floor is not level you could easily end up with no water at all in part of the obstacle. Drive light stakes into the ground on one side, where they will not interfere with any machinery movement. With a long spirit-level, measure from the top of the water at its natural level a round distance in meters or feet to the top of one stake, then cut the stake off at this height. Make a note of the measurement.

43. Constructing a water obstacle.

(a). Basic surveying.

(b). Profiles must be level on both planes.

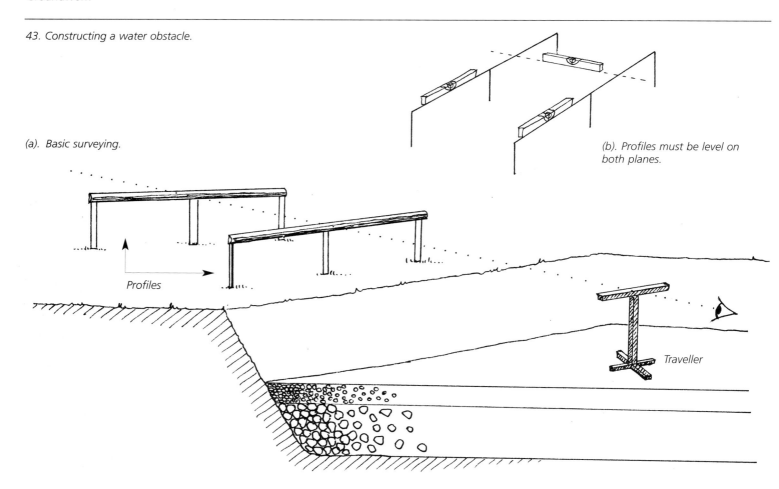

Profiles

Traveller

Level across to the next stake, cut it off at the same height, and work along the other stakes in the same way. Now tack light, straight rails between the tops of the stakes.

Drive in another row of stakes parallel with the first, at least 6' (2m) away, and cut them off to the same height. Fix rails to these as before, or just attach a short 'T' piece to the top of each. If there is room and you have a level long enough, or a laser or dumpy level, it is better to put the second row of stakes on the opposite side of the pond or lake. These reference timbers are called 'profiles'. They will help you to level the stone in the base of the pond. Try not to run over them with the digger!

Now pump out all the water. If the pond has a lot of loose leaves in

*44. Water obstacle. (a). Pumping water out.*

it, they will continuously block the strainer of the pump when the level gets low. To avoid this, dig out some of the leaves and silt to make a sump which is deeper than the rest of the pond and into which all the water will flow. Push some large, clean hard-core into the sump to hold back the leaves, and put the strainer of the suction hose into the middle of it. This will screen out the leaves and allow the water to flow to the pipe.

Pump the water into a ditch or drain if there is one near by. If there is not, pump the water far enough away from the pond to avoid soaking the ground over which you might want to travel with machinery. When using pumps in winter, if they are not running all night make sure that the water is drained out of them, to prevent damage from frost. If the pump is on hire you will be liable to pay for any frost damage. When the pond is empty, do not take the pump away until you are sure that the water is not seeping back in.

If the pond or lake is fed by a running stream or ditch, dig a trench round the pond, then build an earth dam across the ditch downstream of the trench to divert the water into it. Start digging the trench at the downstream end of the pond or lake so that water just flows back up the bottom of the trench as you are digging: you will then have the levels right. If the trench is started at the upstream end, water will gush into it and make digging impossible.

It may be necessary to build a small earth dam at the outflow of the pond, to stop water flowing back in from this end. It can be useful to lay a pipe in the trench before filling it in. It can then be driven over and used to divert the stream again in the future, to carry out maintenance work on the obstacle. If horses are likely to have to go over the trench, fill it in with clean hard-core, compact it thoroughly, and top it off with ¾" (20mm) stone. A loosely backfilled trench with wet earth in it is one of the most dangerous obstacles you could have on a cross-country course. The legs of a galloping horse would sink deep into it, with unthinkable consequences.

By far the best machine with which to construct a water obstacle, both for removing silt and sludge and for levelling out hard-core, is a tracked 360-degree excavator. They come in sizes from 1 to over 30 tons, so choose a size which is appropriate. The most useful implement is a ditching bucket, which is wide, picks up a good load each time, and has holes in it to let excess water out. As it has no teeth, it is also ideal for levelling out the hard-core.

If the excavator is supported by a pair of four-wheel-drive dump trucks, one can be tipping while the other is being loaded, as long as it is a fairly short haul to the tipping site.

These machines are ideal for carrying sloppy material. If you use tractors and trailers, the driver will have to be continually opening and shutting the back door of the trailer, slowing down the travelling time: a dirty and awkward job with liquid sludge! Also, tractors and trailers become stuck much more easily than self-propelled dumpers, as ground conditions always deteriorate when this type of work is going on.

Absolutely all the soft material must be removed, until firm grey-blue clay has been reached. **Note:** Some man-made ponds have a puddled clay lining which is not very thick. Do not dig through this as it may allow all the water to drain away when the pond is re-filled.

The silt and sludge must be replace by a layer of hardcore no less than 18" (45cm) thick. If this cannot be achieved without digging through a puddled clay lining, a membrane such as 'Terram' should be considered. If it is laid onto the clay under the hardcore, a thinner layer

*44. Water obstacle. (b). Removing sludge.*

of stone may be used. Should you dig to a great depth and still not reach a really firm layer of clay, the whole project may have to be abandoned. If, however, the clay is not too wet and soft, a membrane may help to spread out the load of the stone and stop it sinking, which will save the operation. Before starting to put money into a hole which may never be any use, it might be as well to consult a construction engineer.

With a large digger and a small pond, the machine, positioned on the edge, may be able to reach the whole way across and get all the sludge out. If this is not possible, as much sludge as can be reached should be removed, and then large, dust-free 4" to 6" (100 to 150mm) stones put in its place. Drive the digger onto this and track up and down to compact it all. This is where a tracked machine is so much better than one with wheels, as its weight is spread out more evenly over a large area; a wheeled digger's wheels and jack legs will tend to sink into the newly laid stone and rut it. A tracked digger can slew round through 360 degrees and load a dumper directly behind it. A wheeled digger can only slew through 180 degrees, so it has to have room to park sideways in order to dump its load.

44. Water obstacle. (c). Replacing sludge with large hardcore.

Work progressively, a strip at a time, until all the sludge has been removed and replaced by stone. You will now need to use the profiles that you installed before starting the work. To ensure that the floor is level and that the layers of material are the right depth, make a 'traveller'. This is a free-standing T-shaped instrument with a cross – shaped base, which can be made from scrap timber. Its initial height should be the same measurement as the one you originally calculated from the surface of the water to the top of the profile – say 3' (900mm) – plus the depth of water required in the finished obstacle – say 6" (150mm) – plus 8" (200mm), which is the depth of the final two layers of stone, This gives you 4'2" (1.25mm). Tack a T-piece onto the top of the traveller. Stand it on the large hardcore and sight by eye across it to the profiles. If the 'T' is lower than the line between the two profiles, add stone; if it is higher, remove stone. Then check all over the floor to make sure it is correct. Now spread a layer of 2" (50mm) clean stone approximately 5" (125mm) deep. cut 5" (125mm) off the top of the traveller and refit the T-piece. Check all over the floor to see that it is correct. Compact with a vibrating roller or plate compactor.

*44. Water obstacle. (d).Blind over large hardcore with 2" (50mm) clean stone.*

The final layer should be of ³/₄" (20mm) clean, preferably soft, limestone about 3" (75mm) deep. Cut the traveller again to get the level of this material correct. Compact with the vibrating roller or plate compactor.

Every water obstacle must have at least one sloped ramp into it. This is in case a horse is injured in the water and cannot jump out. The ramp also makes it easier to manoeuvre a machine into the pool to clean out silt, and for general maintenance. The ramp must be dug out and

*44. Water obstacle (e). Final layer, clean stone ³/₄" (20mm).*

stoned, as with the rest of the floor: so must any other areas where horses exit, to a distance of at least 12' (3.5m). This is because when a horse exits from water he carries on his legs a considerable amount of water which immediately drains off, and if the ground on exit is not stoned it will soon become badly poached.

If possible, keep a water obstacle free from water when it is not in use. If running water has to be dammed, build a simple sluice with boards in a channel, remove the boards after use, and let the water flow over the floor. When water is slowed down it deposits silt, which will build up in the obstacle and have to be cleaned out annually. All water obstacles should always be emptied out before a competition and any silt removed. Also, check for cans, bottles, bicycle frames, over-reach boots, whips and horse shoes with the nails sticking up!

For steps in and out of water, revetting will have to be carried out in the same way as for other steps or banks. These should always be entirely backfilled with clean stone.

Building a water obstacle where water does not lie naturally may be quite possible in clay soils without using a liner, as long as a reliable and plentiful supply of water is available – but water, which is a valuable commodity, can soak away and evaporate faster than it flows in, especially in hot weather and very dry ground conditions. As it will take many hours – even days – to fill the smallest pool with a domestic hosepipe it is preferable to pump the water from a nearby pond, lake or stream. A land drain or spring may suffice, but it could dry up in the summer.

Dig a test hole, fill it with water, and see how long it takes to soak away. This should be done at the time of year and under weather conditions that are the same as for the competition. If you are pumping from a nearby water source, it is best to run the pump continuously and re-circulate the water through a pipe back to where it came from. In this way the level will always remain constant, the water will stay cleaner, will be moving, and will make a noise, so that the horse will be aware that it is water. The pump should also be running while competitors are walking the course.

A pump with a diesel engine is more economical and easier to get fuel for on a farm, and will run for longer than a petrol engine. A 2" (50mm) delivery hose would just about do for a small volume of water, but a 3" (75mm) is recommended for most jobs. Do keep the pump topped up with fuel, as if it stopped it could give some competitors an unfair advantage or disadvantage.

These artificial obstacles are built in the same way as for a pond or lake except that there is no water to remove first. They always look better if they are not a uniform square or rectangle: multi-sided shapes give you more options of ways to go in and out. Simply dig away the soil to a depth of 18" (45cm) below the eventual desired floor level, and stone up as for a pond. For Pony Club branch events, unless an alternative is provided, the entrance into the water must be a gradual slope with no fence or vertical drop.

If you particularly need to build a water obstacle in very free-draining soil and you have a substantial budget, it is best to use a special pond liner. Ordinary polythene will not work! The area, including the extent of the ramps into and out of the pond, should be measured up and the measurement given to a liner manufacturer who will make up a sheet to size.

The difficulty with this construction is that the liner must have a layer of sand on both sides to protect it from stones. There must also be a layer of hard-core on top, as for all other water fences. The liner must be lost under the ramps in such a way that its edges are well buried and still above water level. It must also be lost behind the revetting of steps. No nails or wires can go through it below water level, so the revetting must be built with its uprights at the back. The front timbers should be bolted to the uprights and the liner up the front, then clad over with timber for protection.

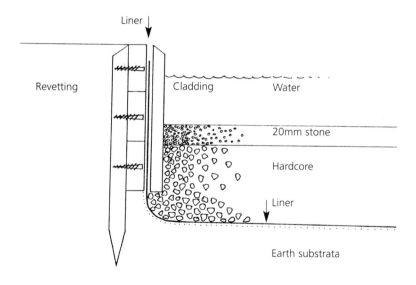

*45. Cross-section showing hard core layers and liner covered with cladding.*

# Other Ground Works

Keeping the surface of the course in good condition is as important as the building of the fences. Horses are increasingly valuable, and rough, hard ground damages their legs and discourages them from performing at their best.

To keep the turf in good condition, mow the grass regularly to about 3" (75mm). This will encourage the roots to grow rather than the leaf. (It is the roots which make the ground springy.)

In the spring, chain-harrow the course to pull out dead grass, and level any molehills. Repair any damage caused by hooves during wet weather. The track between the fences may only need rolling to put back the divots, but do this when it is dry enough for the wheels of the tractor towing the roller not to make marks. The tractor should have either dual wheels or the widest ones available. Roll in the opposite direction to the way the course runs, in order to push the divots back down. Fill the damaged ground close to fences with 3/4" (20mm) stone, and rake it level. The grass will grow back through this and be reinforced for future use.

Rolling and driving vehicles on the course causes compaction, the groundsman's worst enemy. It creates shallow root growth, so the grass cannot reach moisture from deep down, resulting in drainage and drought problems. Use an **aerator**: a machine which cuts slots or punches holes into the ground to relieve compaction; it also cuts the roots of the grass, encouraging new root-growth; and allows the roots to reach moisture from deeper down, thus helping to keep the grass alive in drought conditions.

Badly poached ground that has gone hard before it has been levelled out can be repaired with a power harrow, an agricultural machine for preparing seed beds, found on most farms. If it is set only about 2" (50mm) deep it will level out the rough ground, and given the right weather conditions the grass will grow back again.

If a competition has to be run when the ground is very hard, it is a good idea to put sand down on the landings, particularly of drop fences. Afterwards, be sure to spread this out to allow the grass to grow back. A heavily weighted or vibrating aerator run over the course several times will also take the worst of the sting out of the ground.

Competitors will appreciate the ground being in good condition as much as – if not more than – good fences. If the going is bad they will remember it and take themselves elsewhere the next year.

*46. Turf aerator with rear-mounted, light weight, flat roller.*

# 6 Alternatives, Combinations and 'L' Fences

A whole course of plain one-effort fences would be dull and not very challenging, especially for experienced riders. Fences which can be jumped in more than one place, and those with related elements, have the most influence on the result of a competition. They can also be the most difficult, expensive and complicated to build, and the consequences of a mistake by the course-builder are more dire. Moreover, such fences put the riding ability of the jockey and the course-walking skills of the team trainer to the test as much as – if not more than – the pure physical ability of the horse or pony.

In Pony Club competitions the challenge is to make good alternative fences where time penalties are incurred for jumping the less difficult elements of an obstacle or combination. This is because the optimum time for completing the course is such that it is possible to go the long way round and still get home within the time allowed. It would be wrong to reduce the optimum time as it would encourage children to ride far too fast. In adult competitions the time is tighter, and any deviation from the most direct route will incur time penalties.

In Pony Club competitions an 'L' fence should be used where a difficult obstacle has been built, to give an easier option for less experienced competitors. An 'L' consists of a straightforward version of the fence in question, sited near to it. It can be jumped as an alternative or after a refusal, incurring penalties which will be added to the score.

The most basic form of fence offering an alternative is an arrowhead, which has a narrow rail or palisade in the direct line of the course, either on its own or as part of a combination. The alternative is a longer fence which is either an 'L' or is sited at right angles to the narrow fence and takes longer to negotiate. When building an arrowhead, the minimum width of the narrow section should be 5' (1.5m).

Not many single-effort fences will be difficult enough to require an alternative for any but the most inexperienced competitors. Exceptions to this are trakehners – deep ditches with a rail suspended over them; open ditches; big spread fences; and drops.

Where a time-wasting alternative is to be used, it will work to the best advantage if as much time as possible is wasted, so that the good competitors gain the most advantage and the not so good competitors incur the most penalties. This can be achieved by making two changes of direction for the alternative. A 'T'-shaped fence, where the alternative involves jumping two elements, will have this effect. It is now considered unsafe to have an alternative to a fence at right angles to it on the take-off side. This is because after a refusal a rider might turn the horse to the alternative and try to jump it from a standstill, which could result in a somersault and the horse landing on the rider. Where only one alternative effort is involved, it should be on the back of the fence – possibly angled away from the fence – to prevent a horse coming into contact with it after jumping the quick way. If there is no option other than to put the alternative on the take-off side, it should be a few yards away from the fence and connected to it by an unjumpable obstruction. Otherwise, try to incorporate some kind of natural barrier which has to be ridden round – for example, a tree, a clump of trees or bushes, or a farm building. As long as it is safe, a farm trailer could be used. Colonel Frank Weldon, for many years the course-designer at Badminton, introduced the fashion of using artificial post and rail fences which had to be ridden round to waste time. This practice, now known as 'Weldoning', is better than making an alternative which doesn't take long enough, but is not as desirable as using natural obstacles.

*47. Fence with flagged 'L'.*

*48. Arrowhead.*

*49. Obstacle with two-effort alternative.*

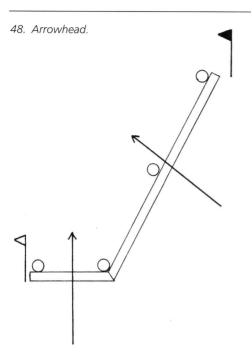

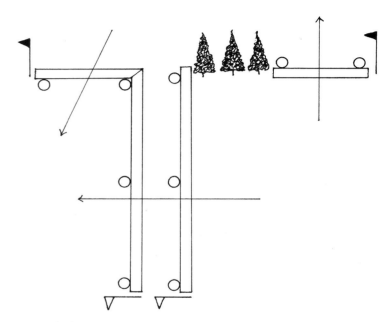

**Combination fences** are multiple obstacles composed of more than one element, and often include alternatives as well as 'L's. There are two types: those with obstacles which are adjacent and separately numbered and judged, and those with lettered elements.

At the separately numbered fences the riders may take whichever course they like in between them, but after a refusal may not retake an earlier fence to get at a later one .

At the lettered combination, only three attempts are allowed at the entire complex before elimination is incurred. Having refused at one element, the rider is free to re-take another, or even to go the wrong way through the flags in order to gain access to the fence at which the refusal took place. If the competitor turns a circle or crosses his track between the elements he is penalised as for a refusal.

Obstacles such as steps should always be lettered, so that after a

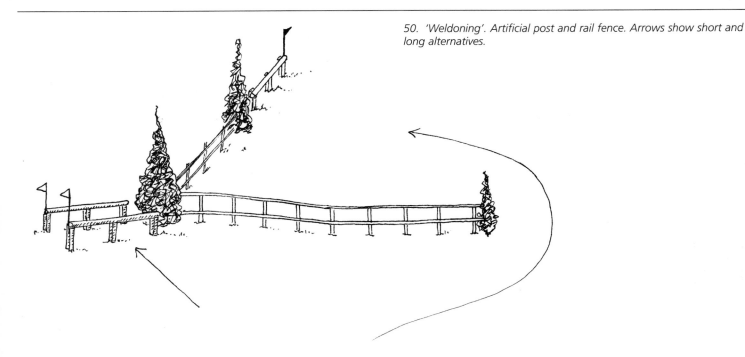

*50. 'Weldoning'. Artificial post and rail fence. Arrows show short and long alternatives.*

refusal a competitor can re-take all of them again without becoming stuck halfway up or down.

The most basic form of combination obstacle is the plain double. This is two fences of any construction, a related distance – either a bounce (no stride in between) or one or more strides – apart.

It is difficult to generalise about the distances between related fences, as there are so many variables – such as the height, the spread, the slope up or down, the size of the horses expected to jump them, and the speed at which they are likely to be travelling. In Pony Club competitions, where there will be both horses and ponies in the same class, always work to the horse distances, as ponies are generally handier and will adapt.

The best way to play safe is to build the elements out of parallel with one another, so that there is a different distance between them

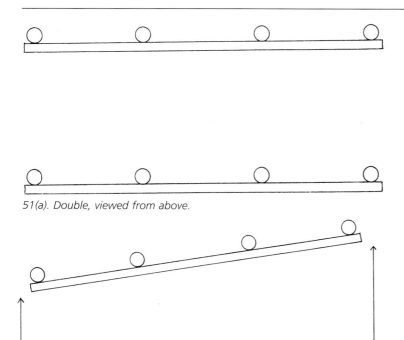

51(a). Double, viewed from above.

21' (6.3m)    27' (8m)

51(b). Angled double, viewed from above.

from one side to the other. For this to work, the elements must be at least 24' (8m) long so that the angle between does not become too obtuse. If in doubt about a distance, take expert advice rather than risk having a problem on the competition day.

- A bounce for horses is between 13'6" and 15' (4 and 4.5m).
- One stride for horses is between 23' and 27' (7 and 8m).
- Two strides for horses is between 35' and 38' (10.5 and 11.5m).
- For more than two strides add 11' to 13' (3.3 to 3.9m) for each subsequent stride.

The distance should be measured from inside to inside of the top of the fences concerned.

A bounce should never be built without an alternative, but *do not* build an alternative on the take-off side of an element at right angles to it. A rail at right angles to each element, on the left of one and the right of the other, will mean that riders have to go through the middle of the bounce and change direction twice – which will take considerable time. The same system can be employed for a one- or two-stride combination, but should only be necessary for novice competitions.

If there is any chance of a competitor attempting to jump the alternative from a standstill following a refusal at the main fence, the alternative should be sited on the back (landing) side of the main route.

To make more complex combinations the elements can be multiplied and set at different angles from one another. Different types of fence construction can be employed for each element.

The next move is to incorporate a **corner** into the complex. This too should always have an alternative. A corner should be built in such a way that the difficulty can be adjusted after the fence has been built. Before you start, lay the poles on the ground and make sure that the

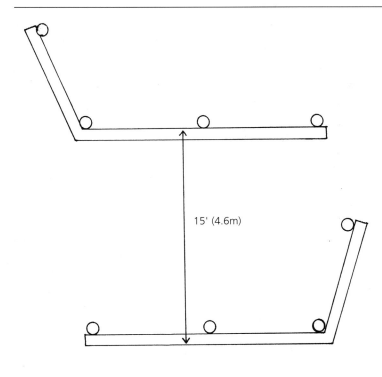

15' (4.6m)

*52. Bounce box showing long alternative including two direction changes.*

site is suitable. The front rail should overhang the end of the back one by about 18" (50cm), making a stubby 'Y' shape.

The spread of the corner should not exceed that allowed for the competition, where a horse can reasonably be expected to jump it, usually not less than 4' (1.2m) from the apex. By laying the rails out you can check this measurement before putting any posts in the ground. The actual thickness of the poles will affect the geometry of the fence, so make sure that those laid out are the ones that will be used; it is no good laying out the obstacle with light fencing rails and then building it with large telegraph poles!

When the layout has been decided on, put one post inside the 'V' and further ones at no more than 8' (2.5m) intervals along the rails.

The most important post on a corner fence is the first one away from the corner on the back rail, as this is where the fence will be hit by a horse making a mistake and getting the corner too wide. Raise the rails and make sure that the back one is clearly visible. It should be about 1½" (40mm) higher than the front rail. At a corner post the force of a horse hitting the back rail will be taken by the rope, so put it round double to give it extra strength.

There should be no lower rail on the first section of the back of the corner so that it will be safer if a horse and rider should end up in the middle of the 'V'. The lower rail of the front should overhang the corner post by the same amount as the top rail.

When the fence is scrutinised by the course inspectors, the amount to be cut off the overhanging front rail can be decided on. Cut off a small piece at a time, and have a flag ready to stand on the end of the rail to give a precise impression of what the fence will look like to horse and rider. Do not cut off too much: err on the easy side for the first use of the fence, as more can always be cut off for subsequent competitions.

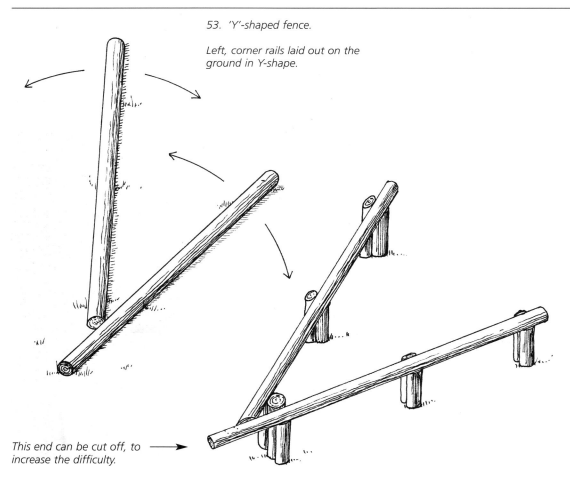

53. 'Y'-shaped fence.

*Left, corner rails laid out on the ground in Y-shape.*

*This end can be cut off, to increase the difficulty.*

On the days when the fence is to be used, stand Christmas trees in the gap between the poles, where it is not safe to jump the whole corner in one and too narrow to bounce, between approximately 6' (2m) and 10' (3m) from the apex.

The rails of a corner can either be lengthened enough distance for a bounce and a stride in between, or a step can be built into the back rail to make a bounce and/or a corner without using such long poles and to make the elements more parallel with one another. Alternatively, a witch's hat shape can be made, with the corner rails only long enough for the corner itself to be jumped, then changing angle to a rail before the first element and one after the second element, in line with one another so that the alternative is time-consuming.

It is unlikely that the right-angled alternative on the first part of a corner will be jumped

110

from a standstill, because horses normally run out at corners rather than coming to a dead stop. However, to be on the safe side, build the alternative a few yards away and join it to the main fence with some Weldoning.

The safest way to build a corner is to table the top in – i.e. to make a solid roof between the two poles, where a horse is likely to jump, which is strong enough for the horse to bank. Then if a rider makes a mistake and asks the horse to jump where it is too wide, a fall is less likely.

**Steps** can be related to other steps or to upright fences. Horses find it easiest to jump when they are going up steps because their hocks are

*54. Corner, with the gap decked-in to prevent a horse falling in-between the rails.*

under them and can push them up over the fence. They find it most difficult to jump a fence after a step down, as their hocks are trailing and not in a powerful position. This configuration of fences should therefore be avoided, except for the most experienced competitors.

Flights of up to about four steps can be jumped up or down. After this number, when going up, horses may loose impulsion and leave their legs behind, or refuse and find it difficult to take the obstacle again. The normal distance between steps is 9' (2.8m), which horses will bounce without difficulty. If a stride is required, the distance should be 18' (5.4m). A step or series of steps up can be followed at 9' (2.8m) or 18' (5.4m) by an upright fence.

This can precede a step down by 9' (2.8m) but it is not recommended, as there is the chance of a horse going too fast, jumping the rail and the step down in one, with unpleasant consequences. It is safest to use the 18' (5.4m) distance for this combination.

A good test of the rider's control is to build a narrow or quite steeply-angled fence at the top or the bottom of a flight of steps. At the top it should be 18' (5.4m) to the middle of the fence from the top of the top step. After steps down, the fence should be at least two or three strides away – that is 21' (10.3m) plus 11' to 13' (3.3 to 3.9m) for each additional stride.

**Banks** can be treated in much the same way as steps. The distances between the step up onto a bank and a fence off are the same as for a step. To make it different a ditch can be dug in front of a bank or a step up.

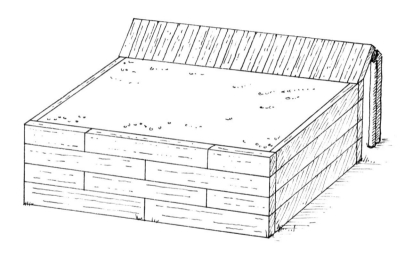

*55. Bank with fence off. The jump off should be half the height of the bank.*

There are two other standard combination fences: **coffins** and **sunken roads**.

**Coffins.** It is not considered politically correct for obstacles to be referred to in the event programme or by the commentator as 'coffins' but the name is still used for identification purposes, as everyone in the sport knows what it means. Basically, a coffin is a ditch at the bottom of a hollow, preceded by a fence – usually post and rails – and followed by a similar fence. Sometimes a half-coffin is built for novice competitions. This has only one fence (as well as the ditch). Where no suitable natural hollow occurs on the course site it has become fashionable to build a coffin-type fence on the flat. This is not a genuine coffin, and riders tend to approach it too fast, so that the distance between the rails and ditch becomes a problem. The correct distance from rail to ditch and ditch to rail is 18' (5.4m) which always works well except when the obstacle is built on the flat, where it is too short for the horses who are going fast.

The most likely part of a coffin to cause refusals is the first element, where the horse sees the ditch just as he is about to take off. This element should always have an alternative – but *not on the take-off side directly attached to the straight way;* as mentioned earlier, this could be dangerous.

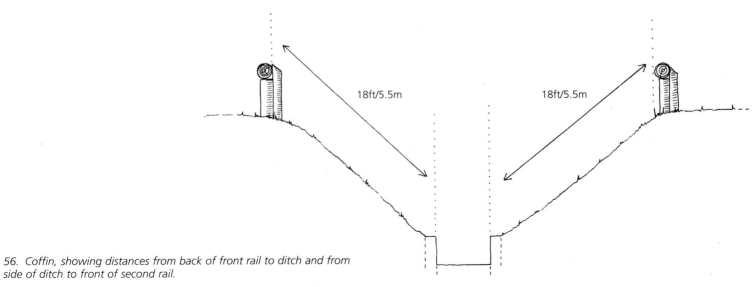

18ft/5.5m     18ft/5.5m

56. *Coffin, showing distances from back of front rail to ditch and from side of ditch to front of second rail.*

**Sunken roads** consist of a step down followed by a step up – usually with a fence before and after. The distance between the first element and the step down can be as little as 10' (3m) as the look of the road should back a horse off and prevent him from jumping the rail-and-step in one. It is surprising how even at this distance some horses will manage to fit in a short stride or shuffle. The *safest* distance is 18' (5.4m), at which all horses will fit in a comfortable stride.

The distance between the step down and the step up that seems to work best is 21' (6.3m). From the step up to the following fence, 9' (2.8m) or 18' (5.4m) can be used. As with the coffin, it is the first element that is most likely to cause trouble, so this is the most important one for which to have an alternative. If short distances are being used, it is vital for the combination to be lettered, not separately numbered, so that a competitor can go back and re-take an element already jumped after a refusal. This also applies to a flight of steps.

Many other configurations of combinations can be built using different fence constructions and incorporating water, ditches, steps and banks: the only limits being the imagination of the course-designer. An obstacle should not be composed of more than about four or five elements. As long as the recommended distances above are adhered to, horses should find all the above combinations jumpable.

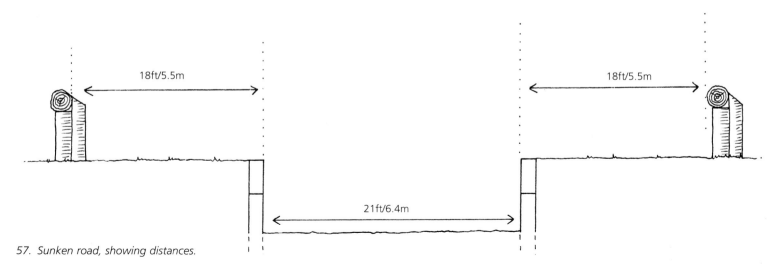

57. *Sunken road, showing distances.*

# 7 Flagging, Crowd Control and Fence Repair

The overall appearance of your course on the event days depends on the final dressing and preparation.

• Use fence marker flags that are tall enough and large enough to set the fences off attractively – at least 6' (2m) tall with triangles at least 1' (30cm) from base to apex.

• Fence numbers should be at least 8" (20cm) square and clearly visible.

• A coat of creosote or equivalent applied each year before the fences are used will smarten them up.

• Narrow fences and island fences will benefit from Christmas trees or bundles of birch on either side to act as wings.

• Parallel fences look attractive with short trees in between the rails, as long as the back rail is not obscured.

• The course will look smart if it is chain-harrowed and rolled. Fence take-offs and landings should have been levelled after previous use. If not, they may require filling in with either stone or sand, depending on the time of year and the likely weather conditions. If the grass is long it may require mowing, and the areas around the fences will have to be strimmed. Make sure to fill in any holes left where livestock fencing has been taken down.

Crowd control. This is very important, even if you are not expecting many spectators. Should someone be knocked down by a horse and hurt in an area where there was no indication of this possibility occurring, the Health and Safety Executive may ask some very searching questions.

At the very least, the start and finish and practice area should be roped off. Use short wooden posts about 3'6" (1.1m) long and 2' x 1' (50mm x 25mm) in section, as these are simple and quick to knock in. Hardwood stakes will stand repeated hammering much better than softwood, which will split after a short time. Plastic electric fencing stakes can be used, but a wooden stake will still be needed at the end of a run or on a corner. Metal stakes should not be used, as they are dangerous if a horse goes through the string and drags them with it, but if there is no alternative, secure the rope or string with elastic bands.

Use thick white bale string, which is cheap to buy and clearly visible. If it is to be re-used, roll it around drums, as if it is simply bundled up it will be impossible to pay out again. Make sure that the string allows riders plenty of room for all the alternatives on the course. Leave plenty of gaps for emergency vehicles and score sheet runners to move around the course.

*58. A fence flagged and dressed with trees.*

**Fence repair.** On competition day the course-builder should arrive early and check that no damage has been done by course-walkers, vandals, stray animals or the wind; also check the water jumps if applicable.

It is important to have a well-equipped fence repair vehicle. As a tractor and trailer are a bit slow for this job, a pick-up truck is recommended – with four-wheel drive if it is likely to be wet. Take all your tools with you. Make sure that the chainsaw is sharp, filled up with fuel and oil, and with the starter cord in good condition. Carry a spare saw if possible. Wear your safety clothing or at least have it ready to put on: you never know who may be watching you from the crowd.

With you in the vehicle should be nails, staples, rope, wire and spare fence marker flags. It is useful also to have a few half-round fencing stakes, which can be used to prop a damaged post, replace a broken palisade slat, or splice over the break in a pole.

If ground conditions are likely to be wet, 20mm stone must also be

*59. Areas roped off for crowd control with thick white bale string.*

on hand (loaded onto a dumper or trailer) to infill any take-offs and landings which become badly poached. Ideally, the stone should be stored under cover, as it will be more serviceable if kept dry.

Keep your walkie-talkie radio with you at all times. Do not leave it in your vehicle when you are attending to a fence or having a meal break. Respond immediately and clearly to a call from the Controller to attend a fence.

Many minor repairs, such as a damaged flag, can be carried out without stopping the competitors. If this is the case, or if you need horses stopped, let the Controller know. It is always preferable not to stop horses already on the course. If the next starter can be held up and any horses already on the course allowed through, this is the best option. If horses are not being stopped, ask the fence judge to alert you when one is coming. Do not leave any tools or materials – such as pieces of wood with nail-points sticking out of them – on the ground by the fence.

If a top rail is broken it is often possible to borrow one from an adjacent fence which is to be used for another class. Should a fence be very badly damaged, consult with the Steward, as it may be best to cut it out of the competition rather than have a long hold-up while it is repaired.

You may have to dismantle part of a fence if a horse has become cast in it. Do this as quickly and as quietly as possible. If the horse starts to struggle, ask the vet to dope him so that he and you and your helpers are less likely to be hurt.

If the course has been correctly built in the first place there should be very little for the fence repair team to do on the day except enjoy watching their handy work being put to the test!

60. *Loading ¾" (20mm) stone for groundwork onto a dump trailer.*

# 8 Health and Safety

The author has incorporated many useful and practical safety tips within the text of this book but it is important for anyone contemplating building a cross country-course to be made aware of the relevant health and safety regulations that cover the tasks being performed, the equipment and substances used and the protective equipment required. This chapter is not concerned with the use of the course as far as the ridden horse is concerned but with the health and safety of those involved in its construction or refurbishment.

Some early words of warning: health and safety legislation changes fast and is far reaching, often being exhaustive in detail. The main objective of this chapter is to draw the reader's attention to the applicable points of the various regulations rather than actually to inform the reader of the detail or the most recent update. This information can be obtained from your local Health and Safety Executive or Environmental Health Office that should be contacted if you have any doubts whatsoever.

## Health and Safety At Work, etc., Act 1974

This is the most important piece of health and safety legislation. Many people mistakenly think they have to be either an employer or an employee for this act to apply. They are very wrong for it also applies to the self-employed and to most voluntary workers. From our point of view the main provisions are those concerning the health and safety of anyone working on a cross-country course, the protection of others against health and safety risks from our work activities, and the control of danger from machinery, equipment and substances that we plan to use.

The more general duties extend to the provision and maintenance of safe plant and systems of work; the safe handling, storage, maintenance and transport of articles and substances; providing any necessary information, instruction, training and supervision; providing a safe place of work, with safe access and egress; and providing a safe working environment with adequate welfare facilities.

Where a person employs five or more people there is an absolute duty to prepare a written safety policy and to ensure it is brought to the attention of all those involved.

## Management of Health and Safety at Work Regulations 1992

Identifying hazards and assessing the risks they pose is one of the most important tasks in the prevention of accidents, and is the main requirement of the Management of Health and Safety at Work Regulations. The method by which it is achieved is known as a 'risk assessment'.

The first stage in carrying out a risk assessment is to identify the hazard (something that has the potential to cause harm) and then to evaluate the risk involved (the likelihood of harm occurring).

For example being entangled in moving parts of machinery is a hazard. The risk will be dependent on how well the moving parts are guarded and how close to it one has to work.

Another example of a hazard is the sawdust created by cutting wood. The risk is whether or not the sawdust will be inhaled. Having established that a hazard and a risk exist the next step is to identify who is at risk and what controls to implement. The best method of control is removal of the hazard (order the timber to size?). Other risk-reducing measures could include substitution with a safer product or system (use a coarser saw to produce less fine dust), enclosure of the hazard or of the people (use a dust extracted saw cabinet or use barriers to keep people at a safe distance), reduced exposure time (don't do all the sawing at once or saw outside, using the wind direction to remove the dust from your breathing zone). In some instances the use of warning signs may be of value (**'Caution: saw bench in use'**). If all else fails, use protective equipment (disposable dust respirator – face mask). This procedure must be carried out for all the tasks involved in building the course, and care must be taken to protect everyone from harm, including members of the general public who may just 'wander over' to see what is happening. Every effort must be made to assess the risks involved throughout the project – but only concern yourself with real risks such as the dangers of using a chain saw or the likelihood of a tractor turning over. Dismiss the minor possibilities such as

catching your finger in the tractor cab door. However, do give consideration to environmental factors such as working on slippery, uneven or wet ground, and make sure that you keep a record on the *'HSE 5 steps to risk assessment'* recording form.

## The Provision and Use of Work Equipment Regulations 1998 (PUWER 98).

Even the most innocent items of work equipment can have lethal consequences if used in a damaged state or used for purposes other than those for which they were intended.

The scope of work equipment under this regulation is extremely wide, encompassing almost any equipment used for work, including hand tools (hammers, knives, handsaws etc.), machinery (drilling machines, circular saws, post drivers etc.), lifting equipment (hoists, lift trucks, elevating work platforms, lifting slings etc.), climbing equipment (steps, ladders etc.) and applies to new, existing and secondhand equipment.

If you are an employer, a self-employed person, or have control of work equipment, you have a duty under PUWER 98 to ensure that the work equipment provided complies with this regulation. Please note that situations where people supply their own equipment should also be covered.

Equipment must be suitable for the work to be undertaken, and used in accordance with the manufacturers' specifications and instructions. If adapted it must still be suitable for its intended purpose. Its selection and use must have regard to the risks to the health and safety of the operator and other persons who may be affected by its use. Regard must be given to conditions that could render work equipment unsafe (i.e. wet ground conditions, steep slopes etc.).

Equipment must be examined before use to ensure that it is undamaged and that all guards and safety devices are in place, with any failings rectified when discovered. This is in addition to the regular maintenance programme, which must be in place for all work equipment and carried out by a competent person.

Information and instruction on the equipment to be used must be provided and, where appropriate, adequate training given. Self-propelled work equipment, including any attachments or towed equipment, must only be driven by people who have received appropriate training in the safe driving of such work equipment.

Portable hand-held chainsaws are very dangerous machines and must be handled with the greatest of care. Under this regulation, anyone using a chainsaw must have received adequate training and be provided with the correct personal protective equipment.

Measures must be in place to prevent access to any dangerous parts of machinery or to stop the movement of any dangerous part of machinery before access occurs.

Anyone contemplating building a cross country-course using more than hand tools such as hammers and hand saws is strongly advised to purchase from HSE Books *Safe Use of Work Equipment-Approved Code of Practice and Guidance' L22*.

## Lifting Operations and Lifting Equipment Regulations 1998 (LOLER)

This regulation deals entirely with lifting operations and equipment and is in addition to the previous regulation, which also applies in full to lifting equipment. The main objective is to ensure that lifting operations are properly planned and executed by experienced or trained people, with the equipment used in a safe manner and, where necessary, examined at prescribed intervals by competent people.

The scope is wide, encompassing any equipment used for lifting (i.e. fork loaders, lift trucks, rope hoists etc.). It is essential for lifting equipment to be adequate in strength for the task, and that its positioning and installation does not pose a danger to the user or other people. All lifting equipment must be clearly marked with the safe working load, and that weight must never be exceeded.

*People* must only be lifted by work-equipment that is specifically designed for that purpose.

It is advisable for anyone who owns or uses lifting equipment to obtain a copy from HSE Books of *'Safe Use of Lifting Equipment – Approved Code of Practice' L113*.

## Manual Handling Operations Regulations 1992

Manual handling injuries are often both painful and long-term and can have serous consequences to the individual concerned.

You should only attempt to manoeuvre loads you can safely handle given the resources on hand.

In particular, always:

1. Assess the load. (Is it heavy, bulky or unwieldy? Is it going to be difficult to grasp? Is it unstable or are the contents likely to shift during handling? Is it likely to be excessively hot or cold? Are the edges likely to be sharp or excessively rough?).
2. Assess the task. (Where is the load going? Can the size or weight of the load be reduced? Can I avoid lifting from floor or ground

level? Can I avoid lifting above shoulder height? Do I need protective equipment or clothing? Do I need assistance?).

3. Assess the environment. (Do I have sufficient space to manoeuvre? Is the work area uneven, slippery or unstable? Do I have to negotiate steps, gradients or any other obstacles? Are the weather conditions favourable? Is there sufficient visibility?).

4. When lifting: place the feet apart with the leading leg forward. Ensure that your feet and hands are well positioned to equate the load. Ensure that you have and can maintain a firm grip. Keep your back as straight as possible. Avoid jerking or twisting movements. Keep the load close to the body.

5. Try to avoid situations where excessive pushing and pulling is required; apart from the risk of physical strain there is always the added risk of slipping.

These guidelines do not replace the requirement to carry out manual handling assessments as specified under *The Manual-Handling Operations Regulations 1992* and the reader is advised to purchase 'Manual Handling' guidance on the regulations from HSE Books L23.

## Construction (Design and Management) Regulations 1994

This regulation, if applicable, would place a duty on the client, client's agent (where appointed), designer and contractor to take into account health and safety during the construction or refurbishment of a cross-country course. The principal objective is to ensure that health and safety is coordinated and managed throughout all stages from conception, design and planning through to the execution of the work including subsequent maintenance and repairs.

It is possible that some of the larger course-building or refurbishment projects could fall within the scope of this regulation, and anyone contemplating such work is advised to contact his or her local Health and Safety Executive or Environmental Health Office before work commences.

## Noise at Work Regulations 1989

Some machinery will almost certainly fall within the scope of this regulation (e.g. chain saws, tractors, diesel fork lift trucks, weed strimmers etc.). Basically, if you find the noise uncomfortable or have to shout to be heard it will be above the level that requires ear protection. If you own or regularly use an item of equipment that appears noisy you must arrange for the noise level to be measured so that the appropriate ear protection can be provided. In the short term you can take advice from the equipment manufacturer or a supplier of health and safety equipment.

## Control of Substances Hazardous to Health Regulations 1999.

It will be necessary to make an assessment of any substances in use that are considered harmful to the health of those involved with the course, whether it is in its construction or use. If weed killers are used, the assessment will need to consider those who may be affected during its application.

The assessment must cover not only those substances purchased (i.e. creosote, petrol, weed killers etc.) but also those produced during the work itself (i.e. sawdust, exhaust fumes etc.). If your work involves ditches or watercourses, you will also need to consider conditions such as Leptospirosis.

The assessment should take into account the substances designated, use and method of application (i.e. wood preservative to be applied with brush), its known hazards (i.e. possible carcinogen) and possible exposure effects (i.e. causes burns) including first aid requirements. Consider where it is to be used, stored and how exposure may occur (i.e. by splashing during use and by handling recently treated surfaces), the people at risk (i.e. operative and people handling treated surfaces), the expected exposure levels (i.e. high during use, low once applied) and the controls required to prevent exposure (i.e. treat wood after handling and in sufficient time for it to dry before competitors walk the course) including any personal or respiratory protective equipment and training that is required (i.e. wear face-shield with chin guard to BS EN 166 ñ C specification, chemical resistant long arm gloves and overalls). Do not forget to include any storage requirements (i.e. keep cool and well ventilated), the procedures to adopt in event of spillage, container disposal, stability of the substance and any reactive substances you may have in use and the procedures you intend to put in place to prevent reaction occurring.

You will find the product information on the relevant health and safety data sheet available from the supplier of the product.

No one should handle products with which they are unfamiliar or have not received training for, and everyone should read the labels of products before use. In particular, the use of herbicides is restricted to operatives who hold certificates of competence in product handling, mixing and application.

Purchased substances must only be stored in their original containers. Under no circumstances should containers hold substances other than that specified on the label or container.

Both permanent and temporary storage facilities must be kept secured and ventilated to prevent fume and vapour build up. Careful consideration must be given to the safe storage and disposal of empty containers, some of which may contain harmful or flammable vapours.

## Personal Protective Equipment Regulations 1992

In some instances the wearing of protective equipment is mandatory (i.e. when using chain saws – safety helmet, hearing and eye protection, safety clothing, gloves, leg protection and chainsaw boots). In other instances it is just common sense (e.g. thick gloves when handling rough timber). Protective equipment must be to BS or EN standard and must offer suitable protection for the task in question. Even without a chain saw it is anticipated that you will require the use of a safety helmet (general head protection), ear protection (combustion engine powered machinery), a safety visor (eye and face protection from weed killers, wood preservatives and flying wire offcuts), dust mask (respiratory protection from sawdust), chemical resistant gloves (hand protection from weed killers and wood preservatives), thick 'rigger' type gloves (hand protection against splinters and pinching), safety boots (foot protection against toe crushing etc.).

## Electricity at Work Regulations 1989

If electrical equipment is to be used ensure it is only 110 volt powered and is used only in the absence of moisture. Great care must be exercised in the positioning of trailing cables. Operators must visually check cables, plugs and sockets of portable equipment before each day's use. Equipment must not be used until defects have been rectified. More formal checks must be made on a monthly basis to include portable appliance testing. Before starting any work a check must be made to ensure that there are no electricity cables either overhead or underground in the vicinity of the work area.

## First Aid and Emergencies

It is inevitable that people will find themselves in situations where they are working alone in remote areas. In such circumstances they should ensure that they do not place themselves in danger and should let someone know of their whereabouts and their expected time of return. It is essential to carry a mobile phone at all times to summon help in an emergency, and to have available an adequately stocked first aid box including sterile water for eye and wound irrigation where clean water is not available.

It is recommended that anyone working on cross-country courses should seek advice from their doctor about Tetanus protection.

There is always the possibility that materials, ground, and especially water surfaces may become contaminated with rat urine which is capable of infecting people with the serious and often fatal condition know as Leptosporosis or Weil's Disease. It is important to maintain a high standard of personal hygiene – keeping cuts and abrasions covered with suitable first aid dressings, and wearing protective gloves when working in high-risk areas.

## Reporting of Injuries, Diseases and Dangerous Occurrences Regulations 1995 (RIDDOR)

If an accident does occur you may be required by law to report it to the Health and Safety Executive or Environmental Health Office.

Action will have to be taken in the case of a fatality or serious injury (i.e. most fractures, amputation, dislocation, loss of sight, most cases of unconsciousness, admission to hospital for more than 24 hours and work-related acute illness), or where a person is unable to work for more than three days (including non work days) or if a doctor diagnoses a work-related disease. Any dangerous occurrence also has to be reported (i.e. collapse, overturning or failure of load-bearing parts of lifting equipment; plant or equipment coming into contact with overhead power lines; electrical short-circuit or overload causing fire or explosion etc.). For more information contact HSE Books (tel: 01787 881165) and ask for a free copy of *'Everyone's Guide to RIDDOR 95'*. **Many of the HSE publications can also be obtained from the Stationery Office (HMSO), tel: 0870 600 5522.**

# Index

walls
    breeze block **77**
    dry stone **76**
water obstacles **93-102**
    artificial  93, 101–2
    excavation  96–9
    falls  93
    laying floor  99–100
    lining  96, 98, 101–2
    sloped ramp  101
    surveying depth  93–5, 99–100
weed killers  122–3
Weil's Disease  124
Weldoning  106, **107**
width of fences  32
wire  31
wood *see* timber
wood stack  72–3

**Y**
'Y'-shaped fence  109–**110**

**Z**
zig-zag  **49**